Dream on !

TARPAPER DREAMS

A True Story

by Jean Humburg

Jean Humburg

Other books by Jean Humburg:
Honk If You Like Canada Geese
Honk Again (If You Liked Canada Geese)

For additional copies:
www.amazon.com/author/jeanhumburg

Inspiration Press
www.inspirationpressink.com
jeanhumburg@inspirationpressink.com

www.facebook.com/jeanhumburgauthor

TARPAPER DREAMS

*I dedicate this book to the memory of
my beloved husband, Woodie,
who made my dreams come true.*

Pals: Walter, Alfred, Jeanie, Sylvia 1929

TABLE OF CONTENTS

PROLOGUE

Looking back, I see my childhood as a web of contradictions. Every silver lining had a dark cloud. Sooner or later, I got everything I wanted but not without a battle, whether it was a new dress for school or having my picture taken at a photo studio. But the thing I wanted most, I never received.

My family was affluent compared to the others who lived around us. I was going to say who lived in the neighborhood, but that wouldn't apply, as there was nothing cohesive between them and us. My parents were able to send a daughter to college during the depression, have us spend summers in the mountains, go to private camp, have music lessons, drive new cars. However, from my early beginnings, I was informed of my parameters regarding who could be my friends and how far I could navigate. I couldn't understand why we couldn't move, even around the corner, so I could be friends with everyone. But, my father wanted the convenience of having the family readily available to assist him in our furniture store. When he wanted his lunch or dinner, all he had to do was to activate the bell on the front door and go upstairs. This self-serving attitude led us to reside in an area well below our standard of living. It wouldn't have made any difference to me as a non-judgmental child, but I had to abide by my father's prejudice and social status.

As you will see in the stories that follow, I went against my father's restraints with imagination and ingenuity, and did just about everything I wanted to do and made friends with everyone who interested me, adults and children alike.

****

In June 1994, while visiting my son in Jersey City, I decided the time had come to revisit my roots. It had been 45 years of avoidance, but now I felt motivated to share this experience with my husband, son, daughter-in-law and two young grandchildren.

For years I coped with nightmares of "coming home" only to find darkness had fallen on a deserted street. The store was closed and no one lived upstairs. I'd awake tearful and abandoned. Now, with the support of my family, I could face the shadows of my past.

We started south from Jersey City over the Bayonne Bridge into Staten Island. It didn't look anything like the countryside I remembered from those many Sundays when we crossed on the ferry to make collections from delinquent customers.

What were once farmlands and cemeteries are now small towns intersected by the Staten Island Parkway. Most of the through traffic was headed for the Verrazano Bridge, the world's highest and longest suspension bridge, which spans the Narrows, the entrance to New York Harbor.

A heavy mist covered the towers as we made our approach onto the slick deck.

"There's a story about this bridge and your great-grandmother," I began, getting the attention of the grandchildren. "Your Daddy probably doesn't know this story either.

"I remember the date of the opening ceremonies of this bridge. It was November 20, 1964 and my mother, your great-grandmother was one of the happiest people there. The bridge had been under construction for a couple of years and she could watch the daily progress from every window of their apartment. This was where they moved to after your great-grandfather retired and sold the business. Sometimes she'd use binoculars to follow the steelworkers high on the cables. Over time she developed a real kinship with this unfolding span. Then, almost as the bridge was finished, Great-Grandmother had a serious heart attack and was hospitalized for five weeks. She prayed she would survive to return home and see its completion."

I could see I had captured the interest of the children so I continued.

"At this time I was living in St. Thomas in the Virgin Islands and couldn't come to see her, but I knew of her love for the bridge. So, I wrote Robert Moses, chairman of the Triborough Bridge and Tunnel Authority and told him about Great-Grandmother. Back came not only a gracious acknowledgement, but an engraved invitation for her to attend the ribbon-cutting ceremony. She was right up there with Governor Rockefeller, Mayor Wagner and the Italian Ambassador to the United States when they let the first cars roll onto her bridge."

GENESIS

As we made our descent off the bridge, I could see a familiar park, part of the Fort Hamilton Military Reservation since Revolutionary days. "I used to play in this park as a child and climb over a big cannon," I said, excitement beginning to well up. "When your daddy was a little boy, I took him there also and he loved it as much as I. At the time, we were living with Great-Grandma and Great-Grandpa for a few months while waiting to join your daddy's father overseas after the war."

We parked the car and walked a short way... and there was the cannon. Memory usually imagines things larger than life but this ancient black cannon was truly immense. In no time, my son and the children were straddling it.

After having lunch at the charmingly restored art-deco Hotel Gregory in Bay Ridge, we toured the tree-lined streets, marveling at the tidy houses and rose gardens. The avenues were broad and peopled with families out for a Saturday stroll. Suddenly a landmark would appear — a Catholic church and school, the Knights of Columbus building, the synagogue, where my father would make a yearly appearance, if it didn't interfere with his day at the track.

We drove by Public School 170, my grade school, and sturdy enough to withstand another 100 years.

My heart quickened as we approached Bay Ridge High School, my cherished alma mater. Here, in this school, I was encouraged by all my teachers to be the best student and citizen I could be. I was in a special class of 35, called the Turner School, and we followed a highly academic curriculum. I had been warned that the school was now a Telecommunications and Technical school for ethnic minorities. Also, a construction trailer was occupying our treasured Senior Garden. However, this imposing architectural grand lady of 83 years still looked beautiful to me.

Immediately adjacent was my mother's church, a Romanesque copy of the Parthenon. I remembered it as having many marble steps leading to the entry, but there were only three. This Christian Science church, where I spent many Wednesday nights asleep on my mother's lap on a hard pew, is now Greek Orthodox. It is enclosed by a wrought iron fence and surrounded by wires of bare light bulbs that probably blink.

The Alpine Theater, my home every Saturday afternoon, is a seven-theater multiplex. Gone are the impressive marquee and the sand-painted front. Four dollars will get you into a cubicle where once for 15 cents you could sit all day in an opulent hall with stars on the ceiling and a crystal chandelier fit for a palace.

At last, we turned down 69th Street and parked across the street from where I once lived. The cobbled streets are now asphalt and the trolley cars no longer crowd the thoroughfare. As I aimed my camera, we were observed by the curious East Indians now occupying the two storefronts where our furniture store used to be.

"This is where I was born. Your daddy was born at Mitchell Field but spent his first year of life above the store. Your great-great-grandmother, Julia, died there, and I was married to your daddy's father a few days after he got his flight wings right in that apartment."

I was relieved to see there was no graffiti, broken windows or iron bars. However, the door leading into the apartment, once glass paneled, looked like the solid steel entry to a bunker.

All kinds of emotions surged through me. I could feel adult rage replacing childhood fears. Just think, I could have lived on any tree-lined street with my own rose garden or even on a bluff overlooking the Narrows with a sloping lawn. I could have had "legal" playmates and sleepovers for my camp friends. I could have had a sense of belonging in a friendly neighborhood. And, I would not have spent years plotting my escape, only to find it by a too early marriage at 18.

Now, I look at my sleeping grandchildren, bored by my day of discovery. I exchange thoughts with my son and husband of 28 years. I reflect on the challenges I've faced and the place where I find myself, in this 70th year of my life. Would I change it all for earlier comfort and jeopardize what I have now?

My path was circuitous, leading me through labyrinths of experiences. It's time to put my anger to rest and celebrate the episodes I encountered along the way. And with the ability I still have to see through the innocence of child eyes, go back to my rooftop and seek out those tarpaper dreams.

Part 1

JEANIE

Chapter 1
SIGNPOSTS

By the time I was ten years of age, my family name was up in lights. It was a twelve foot tall, double sided inverted tee-shaped sign. In keeping with the era of the thirties, it was appropriately Art Deco. The black enamel base with gold fan design at the bottom of each side was a fitting background for the bold, red neon letters. The unbroken threads of nylon tubing read "BROWN" on the twelve-foot vertical section, and continued "FURNITURE — EVERYTHING FOR THE HOME," scripted horizontally.

The sign was bolted to the brick wall outside my bedroom window and it crackled and sputtered from dusk until at least 11 p.m. nightly (except Sunday) or until the last customer departed. Pigeons roosted between the panels, cooing and strutting on my windowsill when not producing offspring. I was forbidden, one of my many childhood "forbiddens," that I ignored, to befriend these birds as they regularly deposited droppings, molting feathers and shells on the awnings below or onto the store entry. Every known pigeon-discouraging method was employed to get rid of these polluters, but much to my delight, it was to no avail. Since they were not going to leave, I chose to continue scattering crumbs along the sill.

As the store was in the middle of the block, the height and dimension of the sign made it visible from Fourth Avenue on the west, to Fifth Avenue on the east. The whole family was made aware that this majestic sign was a symbol of my father's success in business. Now all of Bay Ridge could see Mr. Brown had arrived.

His arrival actually began twenty years previously in 1912. My father was one of twelve children living in a two room house in the village of Kapos in northwestern Hungary where his father ran a flour mill. Despite their living conditions, he never felt deprived of the necessities, but he yearned for more than village life could offer.

At nineteen, with conscription pending, he devised a clever plan whereby he could leave without causing further disruption. Two brothers had already made their way to America without parental permission.

Being blessed with a beautiful, baritone voice, he was able to perform locally in addition to cities as far away as Zagreb. With some of the money he earned, he enlisted the services of a tailor and had him make a tuxedo outfit along with a silk shirt. Then, he bought a pair of black patent leather shoes and a cane with a pearl handle. He gave all his belongings to a younger brother making him promise not to tell anyone until he was long gone.

Being royally outfitted, he bought a first class train ticket. When the guards stopped the train at the Austrian border, my father said he was going to a wedding in Vienna, and looking the part, they let him go through even though he didn't have a passport. He proceeded on to Hamburg where for $40, he boarded the Kaiserin Auguste Victoria for the nine day voyage to America. Needless to say, he was the best dressed passenger in steerage.

By the time he reached Ellis Island, he had 40 cents left in his pocket. The challenge now facing him was to notify his older brother Charlie that he had, indeed, arrived. The trouble was, he didn't have a home address, just that he lived on Houston Street. Methodically, every day, my father sent a penny postcard to every address on Houston Street. After three weeks, a card arrived at a cafe that Charlie frequented and a connection was made. Now, with deportation looming, Charlie finally showed up. Charlie's presence was necessary to vouch for his younger brother's character to the immigration officers and assure them a bed would be provided.

Getting a job was of primary importance, but he had no skills such as Charlie who was working as a clothing cutter. There was no time to take in the sights and sounds of the teeming city. What a contrast it all must have been to this farm boy. My father had taught singing in the villages in his district in Hungary, but he had no idea how to capitalize on this talent.

After attempting to work at a few unsatisfying jobs, he read in a Hungarian paper that auditions were being held at the Manhattan Opera House on 34th Street. When he arrived, he found hundreds of boys and girls lined up outside the stage door entrance all vying for a chance to be part of the new Firefly Company under the direction of Rudolf Friml.

Although he knew no English, he could read music, and someone in the cast helped him sound out the words phonetically. They liked his style and his tones were so melodious, he was hired to play the part of the organ grinder in the new operetta, "The Firefly." When it was time for the programs to be printed, the producer asked my father, "Young man, what is your name?" "Mono Braun," he responded. "Not good," said Oscar." From now on your name is William." So, that is how my father became William Brown, dubbed no less by the impresario, Oscar Hammerstein.

My mother, who, several years earlier, had immigrated to New York with her family, was taking piano lessons from the same teacher who was my father's voice coach. Mrs. Rose, at my mother's insistence, arranged for her to stand behind a screen so she could observe this blond, curly-headed young man with the lovely voice. She found him irresistible. As a result of a subsequent meeting, they fell in love. Unfortunately, before long he was on tour, the hundred-person cast occupying a full train that took them the length of this vast country before ending up in San Francisco. He was gone for almost a year.

Faithfully, love letters written in Hungarian were dispatched, bearing postmarks of towns my mother never heard of. The promised paychecks kept coming and a bank account was beginning to grow along with the romanticism of their situation. By the time the wandering minstrel returned, both were eager to consummate their love. Two obstacles remained, however: one, my mother had come to the conclusion over the months of waiting that she was not inclined to live out of a trunk; and secondly, her mother freely expressed negative feelings about her refined daughter associating with show business characters.

My maternal grandmother was an early feminist. Widowed twice before she was thirty, she took over her husband's tie factory in Budapest and saw to the education of her six children. No day care for my mother and her two sisters. They had a governess. Music and fine sewing lessons were provided for Elvira, Syrena and Margaret. Her sons, Daniel and Ernest were tutored in math and languages. A sixth child, Pauline, was born retarded and cared for by a nurse.

Life was not idyllic, but certainly agreeable. But messages from relatives who had immigrated to America had an exciting appeal to my grandmother. She could sell the factory, move to New York and be assured of continued public education for her children. And, perhaps, there would be advanced medical help for Pauline. The decision finally made, my grandmother booked two second-class cabins aboard the S.S. Rotterdam. She was aware that second-class passengers were not required to submit to examination by immigration, and she knew her youngest would not be permitted to enter the United States otherwise.

My grandmother had strong opinions based on years of self-sufficiency. As part of the marriage agreement, my father's singing career came to a halt, partially due to his future mother-in-law's influence.

Somehow, despite opposition, my father regaled my mother with stories of the beautiful city by the Bay so convincingly, that they left New York and headed west to start a new life without family interference. Two months later, after a stopover in Galveston and aboard a steamer passage through newly opened Panama

Canal, the bridegroom and his seasick, pregnant bride stepped onto the shores of San Francisco.

They set up housekeeping in the Mission District while my father used his ingenuity to create a means of supporting his to-be family. There's a picture on my wall of my twenty-one year old parents standing in the doorway of their delicatessen. My mother is wearing a long, white blouse over a street length black skirt, no doubt to cover up the signs of pregnancy. My father looks happy resting his elbow on my mother's shoulder as they both lean up against the window. He's dressed in black pants and vest and a white shirt with gartered sleeves. The sign over the awning reads, "This Place Has Changed Hands and will now be conducted as a First Class Delicatessen Store. Hot Meals 11 a.m. to 7 p.m. Fine Cooking a Specialty." This endeavor was destined to fail. My mother was never a specialty cook, and my father chose the wrong location. He had researched the main arteries for the up-coming San Francisco Exhibition of 1915 and rented the delicatessen that would be directly in the path of the entrance. However, the planning gurus decided on another thoroughfare and left the young couple with lots of uneaten potato salad.

The year my sister, Violet, the first of three children, was born, my father was a salesman for a Business Suit Club. His territory was Pullman, a town across the Bay where the parlor cars were

9

built. He rode his bike from the Mission, boarded the Oakland ferry and cycled to the plant every payday. First he sold the merchandise from a catalog, had the buyer sign a contract, and collected fifty cents a week until full payment was made.

Three years passed and my mother was very lonely. She missed her family especially now that she had a young child. She could see their living situation was not improving, and she begged my father to consider returning to the east coast. There were frequent disputes and one evening when my father returned from work, there was a letter on the kitchen table. My mother had packed her things and taken my sister on a five-day train journey back to New York.

Devastated, my father followed in pursuit and promised to take care of his wife and child in a reliable manner. He was hired as a furniture salesman and remained in the business thirty-five years.

In 1922, my father decided to leave the confines of Manhattan and strike out on his own to the country suburb of Bay Ridge, Brooklyn. It was the new frontier, having just been opened by the extension of the BMT subway line. City lots were sold at auction, and one of the lucky bidders was my father.

He had saved enough money for a down payment on a small brick building that had a storefront, a minuscule apartment in the rear and an apartment above. They lived on the next street while construction was going on, and it was here my brother, Laurie, named after the hero in Little Women, was born. My sister was eight years old.

Soon there were seven other identical buildings and the row looked exactly like Edward Hopper's painting EARLY SUNDAY MORNING.

There was a barbershop with a striped pole, a laundry, a tavern (which later became a speakeasy), a paint store, a candy store, a tailor shop and a tropical fish store. Cold-water flats sprung up on either side of this oasis and across the trolley-tracked street. This was the center, though not the circumference, of my childhood. I loved the commerce of the street and came naturally to it, as I was born behind the furniture store, coincidentally early on a Sunday morning.

Our family life revolved around the store. My parents were partners in the business. My father took care of all the important transactions, and my mother's job was to be available to relieve my father so he could go to the bank, out on collections or a myriad of other excuses he could find to break up the thirteen-hour workday.

Since my mother was always on call and also had to care for my ten-year-old sister and my nine-month-old brother, it was no surprise she was bewildered when she found herself pregnant again. It occurred to her to terminate the pregnancy, but a dear friend said to her one day, "Elvira, what if Mary had decided not to have Jesus." With this weighty statement to lean on, my mother resignedly awaited the birth of her Christ child.

The Bay Ridge Sanatorium was a block away, and therefore made it less imperative to my mother's way of thinking, to report to the hospital after heavy labor had set in. There was plenty of time. My father knew by now that he couldn't possibly make it to the garage and back in time, so he threw all caution to the wind and called a taxi. But by this time I was already through the birth passage. My father was screaming for my mother to keep me in place until we could get to the hospital. I was actually born before we entered the checkered cab that raced us around the corner to the waiting doctor.

I'm sure my bouts of claustrophobia are due to the inability to enter the world when I was ready. I spent the first three months in colic, getting even, no doubt, at my parents for my tardy entry.

A week later, I was brought home in swaddling clothes to the minuscule apartment behind the store. There were two bedrooms, a family kitchen and a small backyard. My crib was in my parents' room along with an oak, upright piano. My father still wanted music around him and was even willing to listen to my mother's choppy Chopin. On rare occasions, my father would have my mother accompany him as he sang songs from operettas in which he performed while working for Rudolf Friml. I was three or four when I first remember hearing these concerts.

Despite our modest dwelling, my mother insisted on having a cleaning lady. It was difficult to wait on customers with one babe in arms and another at her skirts. I remember being fed in my highchair by Olga, a rotund, pleasant Norwegian lady. She often left me in my chair long after I needed to be to keep me out of trouble.

I'd toddle after her to the backyard and watch as she hung out the week's wash. Regularly, the laundry man's German Shepherd from next door would jump the fence, crashing through the clothesline, muddying the whites. My father was convinced this was a ploy to get our business. A feud resulted and as a consequence, Shirley Sanderson, the laundry man's daughter, became an outlawed friend. She was first on the list my father deemed unsuitable. Somehow, despite his wishes, I made sure each one in time became a cherished playmate.

When I was four years old, we bought the adjacent building from the barber and doubled the size of the store. We moved upstairs to a five-room apartment and my maternal grandmother moved in next door. The family was now complete.

Chapter 2
COME AND BUY

I first met customers in my mother's arms. I learned to crawl then walk amid the crowded forests of polished wooden objects. I explored the drawers of a credenza and sometimes ended up on a plump sofa for a nap.

I remember the smells of the store, especially the days the repairman came. He'd set up his little burner with its hissing blue flame and melt the colored sticks to fill the cracks in the wood. The acrid odor permeated the air. He'd work all day and finish the restoration with a coating of oil, making the piece better than new.

For the holidays, the window dresser appeared, and in stocking feet jammed the windows with piles of merchandise. No artistry involved, just the ability to display as many items as possible. Painted signs were posted on each piece of furniture, none over $10.98. I'd play a game with friends; our sticky hands all over the glass panes, to see who could guess which price card had been picked.

As soon as I knew my numbers, sometime in the second grade, I became acquainted with the store's code. It was COME AND BUY, ten letters that corresponded with the first ten numerals. A code signifying the wholesale price was written on a cardboard tag and attached to each item. I was taught to decipher the code MYY to read $3.00, double it and add 98 cents. The price of the sewing table was $6.98. Of course, my father could make any adjustments he chose, either a lower figure for a good customer or higher for a more affluent looking person.

This was important to know, because when we moved upstairs a bell was installed in our kitchen. If the store were left unattended, a switch on the front door would be activated, causing the bell to ring loudly. Meals were hasty or lengthy affairs, as the trick was to finish before the inevitable interruption. Sometimes, dinner would go on for hours, as we had to wait until my father completed a sale. We children were required to remain at the table until excused. My brother and I took turns going downstairs to "see who it is". We'd gather as much information as we could remember and give the price, when asked. If it was an inquiry (or a "queery" as my brother and I joked) or a stray dog, we could continue our meal. Using the code, occasionally, I sold an end table or two.

On Saturday nights, my father brought up a brown paper bag filled with the day's receipts. I'd arrange the bills, making sure all the presidents' heads were in the same direction. He'd total up the receipts and take the same paper bag to the night depository in the bank at the corner.

There were three part-time employees. Fred was the deliveryman and a good friend of mine. I wasn't allowed in the basement, but if Fred needed to bring up a kitchen table or mattress, I'd sneak down the creaky stairs behind him. Cellars are interesting places, no matter what's in them, but especially when you can collect a few pieces of coal from the bin.

Gladys, the bookkeeper, came three days a week. She was a heavy-set, young woman who had constant body odor. I couldn't understand how my father, an immaculate dresser, could stand to have her in the office. I was never able to talk to her, as she warned me she'd lose her place in the ledger.

My favorite was Mr. Winston, the accountant. He always took time to share a joke with me or ask about school. He'd watch me come into the store for my daily hit on my father for a penny to buy candy. It was Mr. Winston who taught me a life lesson.

"Your method is all wrong, Jeanie," he said one day. "This is the way to do it. Pick a time when your father is with a customer and ask as sweetly as you can, 'Daddy, please may I have a nickel?' Don't waste your time asking for pennies when a nickel would be just as easy to get."

You know, he was right!

Chapter 3
VIGNETTE OF SPRING

When you're a child of the city, the harbingers of spring are not so easily detected. There are no robins or daffodils to give you a clue. Yet the signs are nonetheless unmistakable. Suddenly the street vendors reappear after a long absence, resoundingly hawking their wares. They offer farm fresh vegetables, scissor sharpening and sometimes the miracle of a traveling merry-go-round.

It was an unusually bright spring day late in April. Despite the unexpected warmth, I was still wearing ribbed lisle stockings under my woolen jumper as I played "potsy" on the sidewalk in front of my family's furniture store. The striped tan and white awnings were rolled down to protect the window display.

I found I had to hop sprightly between the chalk marks to avoid the scurrying noonday crowds coming from the corner subway. Two trolley cars passed mid- stream and clanged a greeting to each other. Just then I saw my mother approach Mr. Alfonso's vegetable cart. She purchased a solid head of green cabbage and a crinkly cauliflower to take upstairs to our apartment. By afternoon, the house would smell of spicy Hungarian cabbage rolls or overcooked cauliflowerettes, neither of which I was eager to consume.

I ran up to her and tugged on her skirt. "Mommy, please, please, can I ride the merry-go-round?" I pleaded. "It's only a nickel and it's my last chance until next time."

She took a coin from the change in her apron pocket, as she knew she wouldn't be able to resist this persistent five year old for very long. "Just one time around, and don't go bothering your father for another ride," she said, smoothing my hair. "Then come up for lunch."

"What a lucky day," I mused as I climbed the iron steps of the mobile merry-go- round for the second time. This mechanical wonder on a flatbed truck came to our neighborhood when the days were warm and agreeable and brought music and color to the children. There was room for eight small riders on the carousel horses. I headed for my favorite pony, the one with the gold saddle and blue glass studs. I put my fingers through the metal mesh as the driver started to crank the machine. The grinding gears soon blended with the street noises and all I could hear was the strains of "O Sole Mio" carrying me to an enchanted land.

All too soon, it was over. As I descended onto the sidewalk, I noticed a big van had pulled up in front of the store. Though it was not an unusual occurrence, it was sometimes interesting to see what was carried out. Fred, my father's delivery man, was already helping to unload when I skipped up and found myself a safe viewing place. After being warned many times in the past, "Get outta da way, kid," I knew enough to stay clear.

Today, however, as the last item, a small crate was being lifted down. Fred called, "Jeanie, come here! Don't you want to watch me open this one? Could be a surprise for you."

I eagerly watched him peel the slats one by one with his crowbar; never dreaming the treasure to be unveiled could be mine. At last, there it was. My child-eyes could not believe what they beheld — a shimmering chariot with glistening steel handlebars and a black leather seat. Did I say this was my lucky day? It wasn't even my birthday yet, what good fortune could have made me the recipient of such a glorious red tricycle?

With heart pounding, I raced into the store, interrupted a sales negotiation and threw myself at my startled father. "Daddy," I blurted, "Thank you a million times. I love it! I love you!"

I dashed out into the sunshine to take my tricycle for an inaugural ride — only to find it was nowhere to be seen. In the few minutes I had left it unattended, someone had snatched not only my chariot, but also a part of my childhood. I cried for days. My father didn't scold me for being careless, but neither did he offer to replace it.

This taught me early on how fragile and fleeting joy can be.

Chapter 4
JIMMY DA WISE GUY

Holstein's ice cream parlor and luncheonette was around the corner from where I lived. There, I rewarded myself for a good report card or celebrated when I found my piggy bank was on the plus side.

The parlor was situated at the BMT subway lines' 69th Street station. Here, early morning commuters would buy their newspapers, leaving their money in an unattended cigar box before they disappeared into the bowels of the earth. Then, like moles, they'd emerge about 5 p.m. and buy the *Five Star Final* from the same newsstand.

As you entered the parlor, you stepped onto sparkling, white, tile floors — freshly mopped and still smelling from Lysol. On the right stood a mottled, black marble counter in front of eight backless, rotating stools. A long etched mirror graced the length of the wall facing the counter, featuring luscious pictures of mammoth ice cream delights overflowing their frosted containers. Several maroon leather booths lined the other wall.

One day, I was feeling particularly flush, as I had accumulated all of fifteen cents. I could almost taste the smooth vanilla ice cream sliding down my throat as I made my way around the corner. I eagerly pushed open the door and made my way to the nearest stool. Because of my stature, I had to place both feet on the polished foot bar, grab hold of the counter with both hands and pull myself upright.

As I was about to place my order, I heard a voice say, "Hey, watacha name, little goil? I seen ya here a couple of times."

Never having been told not to talk to strangers, I replied dutifully, "My name is Jeanie. What's yours?"

"My friends call me Jimmy da Wise Guy, and I'd like to buy ya a sodah."

I scrutinized the man carefully, noting his straight blond hair slickly combed back and his watery, kind blue eyes. He was wearing a tweedy coat sweater and knickers that buckled over plaid socks.

"No thank you," I heard myself reply — my good upbringing coming through. "But, I really am not supposed to take money from people I don't know."

"Well, ya know me now, 'cause I'm ya friend. I made a little extra money on the horses and I'd like to share it wid ya."

Over the next few months, I got to know more about Jimmy da Wise Guy. He told me he was a bookie who made his office in the last booth from the door at the ice cream parlor. He had permission from the owner, who got a percentage of the take. I didn't understand all this, but I accepted the fact that my being treated to ice cream was determined by how the ponies ran at Belmont.

Jimmy da Wise Guy also became my financial planner. It was getting close to Halloween and I was making fewer trips to Holstein's.

"Haven't seen ya for a while, Jeanie," he said when I came in one afternoon. "Watcha gonna do for Halloween?"

"I'm going to use an old sheet and be a ghost as I always do, and carry a paper bag for my treats. I stay around our store, although my father doesn't like me bothering the customers."

"Listen to me, kid. Do like I say and you'll make a fortune," he insisted. "Get ya mudda to buy ya a witch's hat and a big cardboard pumpkin. Den come stand by da subway when all da people come home from woik and in an hour, you'll be rich."

On Halloween eve at 5 p.m., unbeknownst to my parents, but known to Jimmy da Wise Guy, I was at my post at the BMT. I was wearing a black witch's hat and holding an orange pumpkin. I never even had to say "Trick or Treat!" Yet, to my amazement, the pumpkin filled with clinking coins — and in less than an hour (I had to get home for supper or I'd be spanked), as promised, I was truly rich.

Chapter 5
SYLVIA DUCK AND THE JABESIDO

Sylvia "Duck" was the perfect friend. She was two and one half years younger than I, and we started palling around when I was five. Her uniqueness was her unquestioning loyalty. Her surname was Ducker, but I called her Duck because she would waddle after me wherever I went. She always wore a big beret to protect her head from the wind and sun. You see, she remained quite bald until the age of four.

A trip to the candy store was one of my dailies. Since allowances were unheard of, I had to plead my case every day after school. From Mr. Winston, the store's accountant, I learned the most expedient and efficient way was to wait until my father was involved with a customer and then make my approach. It was smart business to pay up promptly. Coin in hand, I'd skip the four doors down the street and enter that sweet smelling haven. Sylvia's grandfather, Zadie, ran the store while her father drove a big delivery truck for Russell Stover's candies. I never knew my grandfathers, so along with my belabored purchases of a penny's worth, I'd get in a good visit.

Every day Zadie wore the same pinstriped pants and vest. His white, starched shirt studded at the neck was collarless as he had a large carbuncle the size of a baseball. He'd shuffle along the rough, planked floor in worn leather slippers from one glass case to the other, as I'd make my selection. Then, patiently, he'd fill the small white bag and put in a few extra "nigger babies."

When I was in second grade, I convinced Sylvia that we should form a club, just the two of us. We would meet twice a week, Tuesdays at her house and Thursdays at mine. I was to be president and she could take care of the dues — a penny each time we met. The person whose house we used would choose the program for that afternoon. If the junior member couldn't think of anything exciting, the president could make a recommendation. Now, all we needed was a name. Our initials were J.B. and S.D. I was just learning my vowels and inserted the first four between our initials and behold, the JaBeSiDo.

I decided our aim was self-improvement. I drew up a chart similar to the one in Hygiene class, and first thing we did each meeting was to check off tooth brushing, baths and what vegetables we had eaten. We played Pick Up Sticks, Tiddley Winks, had tea parties with miniature cups and saucers, cut out paper dolls and went on picnics to Owl's Head Park. Some

Thursdays we'd meet in my playhouse on the roof. I'd go to the library and choose books I could read aloud to Sylvia. I taught her how to cross-stitch and how to color within the lines. She was a very apt pupil and took directions willingly.

One winter afternoon, being housebound for several meetings, we had run out of things to do. What we needed was inspiration. I brought out two pads and sharpened pencils. Then, I recommended (it was Tuesday and we were at Sylvia's house) that we each draw what we knew of the male and female anatomy.

To my surprise, Sylvia rebelled! How strange it seemed that the longer and thicker her hair grew, the more independent Sylvia became. I was even beginning to doubt her loyalty. The JaBeSiDo was in jeopardy. After that, we gradually disbanded and divided the accumulated dues, none of which had been spent over the years, frugality being part of the program. We remained good friends through high school. I let her know I was always available to give advice, but somehow Sylvia Ducker never asked.

Chapter 6
MRS. LUINETTI

Whenever I see sunflowers growing in a field, looking like blond, adolescent girls whose heads have grown too large for their slender bodies, I think of Mrs. Luinetti. She was my first adult friend, and I adored her with all the passion a six year old could muster.

Our meeting was not by chance, but by the concurrence of two events.

From my second story rooftop vantage point, I could peer directly into my neighbor's backyard and observe the activities below. It seemed to me that summer a phenomenon was taking place right before my eyes. Why, just a couple of weeks ago, those stalks looked perfectly normal growing midst the corn and tomatoes. But now, they appeared tall enough and strong enough to take Jack in the Beanstalk clear up to the sky. What's more, I had never seen such mammoth daisy petals before.

Lately, I'd been noticing a lady in a straw hat using a watering can to tend the small plot. She'd make many trips back and forth through the cellar door to refill the can. I was tempted a few times to call out and ask her about those giant daisies, but I didn't have the courage.

One day, she left her first floor kitchen window open. The sounds of "caw, caw" and raucous screeching penetrated the air. What could that be? Finally, my curiosity got the better of me. I had to find the answer to the two mysteries of the giant daisies and the piercing noises. So, the very next time I saw my neighbor, I called out, "Hey, lady, can I come visit you and see your garden?"

She looked up startled to see a small child on the roof above. There stood, a stranger with a Buster Brown haircut and dark eyes peering out from under overgrown bangs. She must have wondered at the request.

"I guess it's okay . . ." the lady replied. "If it's okay with your mother."

Wanting to take immediate advantage of her offer, I scurried back through our kitchen window, dashed down the stairs and out the front door onto the busy street. I ran towards the building where my neighbor lived, and then stopped suddenly as I approached the stoop. I was scared. I hadn't asked my mother's permission, and I wasn't supposed to enter other houses on the block. I was now facing one of the many grey brick cold-water flats where the Italian immigrants lived. They were poor, and I heard tales of rats inhabiting the baby carriages in the halls.

I slowly climbed the stoops eight steps, counting as I went, hoping to delay the inevitable. It took my whole body weight to open the heavy oak front door, and I catapulted into the vestibule. I stood looking at the gray, tin mailboxes; not knowing which black button buzzer at its top belonged to the lady. So, I took hold of the glass knob of the inner door and found myself in a hallway so dark I couldn't make out the wooden banister directly in front of me. I hit my forehead on the railing and was ready to make a speedy retreat. But up ahead, I heard the now familiar "caw, caw" and bravely decided to go forward.

I was greeted by an overwhelming aroma which I later figured out was a combination of garlic, green peppers and tomatoes. This smell never changed over all the years I continued my visits.

The floorboards under the cracked linoleum squeaked beneath my feet. I slid my hand along the metal moldings on the wall so I could find my way to the door at the end of the hall.

"This must be it," I surmised and held my breath as I knocked softly.

Shortly, the door opened wide and there stood a dim figure brightly outlined by the sunlight behind her. The lady was tall and slim with an elegant bearing. She was clothed in black from head to foot in traditional widow's weeds. Her wiry black hair, the consistency of steel wool, was pulled back severely from her high forehead. Even in the dark, I could see her sparkling jet black eyes under bushy eyebrows. My heart was pounding as I looked up at her. The light had created an aura around her that reminded me of a mosaic saint I had seen on a church wall. Bending down, she took my hand and said quietly without the slightest Italian accent, "Won't you come in?"

"Come in, come in," squawked a high-pitched voice, echoing the lady. There, between two tall, lace covered windows, I could see a large, domed brass cage. Sitting regally on a perch was a magnificent parrot, right out of my jungle picture book. Emerald green velvety feathers covered his back and wings which were outlined in crimson as if by an artist's brush. His head was a crown of royal blue and a yellow breast completed the palette of brilliant colors.

"This is Caruso, my parrot," said the lady. "And my name is Mrs. Luinetti."

Thus started an unusual friendship that began when I was six years old and lasted for seven years of my childhood.

Caruso was a bilingual bird that sang Italian folk songs, whistled Sousa marches and chatted in English just as well as in his mother tongue.

That afternoon both mysteries were solved for me. The tall daisies in the backyard were sunflowers that provided food for the parrot. In subsequent years, I would help Mrs. Luinetti pluck the tightly packed seeds out of the blooms and spread them on a tray to dry. Then, Caruso and I would share in the harvest.

My first visit was brief.

"I'm so glad you came today," Mrs. Luinetti said as I prepared to leave. "You can come anytime, but if I am busy, I will tell you."

Sometimes, I would spend an entire afternoon, other times it would be for only five or ten minutes, but she never sent me away.

Even today, I can see her tidy railroad flat clearly. As you entered the kitchen, the largest of four rooms, the first thing you noticed was the black cast iron wood stove. Something odorous was always boiling in a pot. A white enamel topped table sat in the middle of the room usually covered with yards of material. Near the window, adjacent to Caruso's cage, I can remember an open sewing machine on which Mrs. Luinetti kept spools of rainbow-hued thread. In a corner, a voluptuously padded mannequin stood haughtily. I was careful to avert my eyes if she wasn't properly draped.

A wall of multi-colored glass beads separated Mrs. Luinetti's son Joseph's room from the kitchen. I rarely saw him as I tried to be gone before he came home from work. I was fascinated by the tinkling, rippling sounds that wall created as Mrs. Luinetti passed through. Beyond that, a set of brocade curtains partitioned her bedroom. And facing the street, I was told, was a parlor I saw only once.

There were no windows in the apartment other than front and rear and since it resembled a boxcar, it was commonly known as a railroad flat.

Mrs. Luinetti was a seamstress. Over her black garb, she wore brightly patterned aprons studded with threaded needles like medals of Honor. She sewed for the neighbors, mainly for special occasions such as funerals and weddings. How I envied the little girls who had frothy communion dresses her skilled hands had made for them. And oh, those flower decked veils! I wondered what it would take for me to become a bride of Jesus.

What pleasure it was on rainy afternoons after school to sit by the warmth of the wood stove and straighten out the button box. I can still hear the whir of the sewing pedal and the hiss of the iron as the steam hit the pressing cloth.

The first time Mrs. Luinetti offered me a scrap of velvet, I stroked its downy surface and smoothed it over my cheek. In time I amassed a collection of swatches of silk, taffeta, crepe de Chine, lace — whatever she happened to be working with. I kept a treasure box at home filled with cloth and pieces of satin ribbon. And when there was no work, she'd let me choose from the button box.

As I grew older and developed other interests, I didn't visit my friend as often. It began to seem childish to talk to a parrot and spend time with a seamstress who gave me bits of fabric. I was becoming a young woman of thirteen and graduation from P.S. 170 was only a few months away. We were to wear long, white dresses as was customary in our school system.

My mother and I shopped diligently for the pattern and the perfect material. As we were buying yards of white organza, I slid my hands over the silky surface.

I knew what I wanted to do.

"Mother, would you mind very much if Mrs. Luinetti made my graduation dress?" I asked, knowing my mother assumed she would be the one to do it.

"I know how patient she must have been all these years having you bother her," Mother said. "But now she might be honored to do this for you — strictly on a business basis, of course. Yes, dear, go ahead and ask her."

Mrs. Luinetti made me the most beautiful graduation dress — prettier than any worn by those brides of Jesus. She ignored the pattern and together we created a dress to dream about.

"Let's have a sweetheart neckline and put ruching around it. We'll double layer the skirt," she said, her mouth full of pins. "And how about puffed sleeves? Around the waist, we'll put streamers of pink satin ribbon!"

On the day I came to pick up my dress, Mrs. Luinetti invited me to go back down the hall and enter by the front door that led into her parlor. "This has to be something really special," I reasoned. It was an amazing room compared to the other parts of the flat. Most of the furniture must have come from Italy as it was so ornate. There were damask drapes, a tapestry rug, silk-fringed lampshades and even an oil painting of Venice on the wall.

She asked me to sit on one of the small over-stuffed horsehair chairs.

"Jeanie, I was so happy to be able to make your graduation dress. It will be my going away gift," she began. "My son, Joseph, is finally getting married. He has bought a house in New Jersey and he and his wife have asked me to live with them. I will now have hot water and a bathtub. Can you imagine — even steam heat and a gas stove! And what's more, there is a garden where I'll be able to grow sunflowers for Caruso."

I could feel tears welling up but they had to be of joy. My friend deserved this after all the years of hardship.

When I came home from summer vacation, Mrs. Luinetti had already moved. I kept my treasure box of buttons and scraps for a while, but eventually discarded it along with other remnants of my childhood.

The older I become, the more I cherish the thought of our friendship. Perhaps that is why whenever I see sunflowers growing in a field, I think fondly of my good friend, Mrs. Luinetti.

Chapter 7
THE UGLIEST DOG IN BROOKLYN

During the Depression years, when customers were unable to pay their bills, the antiquated system of barter came into play. My father was a master of the game.

On Sundays, he would drive up in the old navy blue Buick with the mushrooms from the dampness growing on the padded ceiling and announce we were all to go for a drive. This was the day to collect delinquent bills. The deliveryman, Fred, did most of the collections but the difficult ones whose next step was repossession, he turned over to the boss.

My brother and I detested these outings. The trip was always longer than expected. Invariably we would get lost, blow a tire or the radiator would overheat. My pleas of hunger, thirst or "I've got to go to the bathroom, NOW!" would fall on deaf ears. The journey would continue until, by pure chance, we'd pull into the right driveway. A father never asks directions, I discovered early in life. That would be admitting a defect in character.

From the far reaches of Long Island, on one trip, we redeemed several freshly slaughtered chickens and a crate of eggs. The customer could now have her sofa a few more months. A refrigerator, facing its last installment, yielded a case of homemade wine and jars of spaghetti sauce. An Italian maestro traded a year's worth of violin lessons, which my brother used, so his wife could keep the bedroom suite. If it were up to me, I would have begged the maestro to forego the lessons and the furniture would be his.

Margit, our Norwegian cleaning lady, came three times a week to wash, iron and scrub. I don't know what she could have bought to incur two years of indebted servitude. But, when her time was up, Margit agreed to stay on as she had become part of the family.

One particular Sunday turned out to be a profitable one for me. Somehow, we had successfully arrived at a farmhouse in the wilds of Staten Island. I could see my father on the front porch negotiating with the lady of the house. A deal was surely in the making.

"She's sairtenly a foin pup," bragged Mrs. O'Brien. "Best of the litter of these pedigreed toy bulls."

We were all tired, as I could see no other reason why my father, a tough negotiator, would have given in to this level of barter. He returned to the car with a half smile on his face and a bulge in his right pocket. He opened my side door and dropped something squirming into my lap. In exchange for the last five dollars owed on her kitchen set, I now owned a six-week-old puppy. It wasn't long, however, before we realized she was far from pedigreed — "a frankfurter burned on both sides", I used to say — but by that time, it was too late. I was in love with the ugliest dog in Brooklyn.

I called her Bootsie, an obvious choice as she had four white paws. Uncle Charlie thought Nira was appropriate after the National Recovery Act, but he was voted down. Despite my loud protestations, it was debated whether to have her tail shortened as was customary for her breed. We finally agreed it would only make her little body look stranger. Bootsie must have appreciated that decision, as she wagged and thumped her white-tipped tail at every opportunity.

When she was full grown, she was given a plaid coat with a silver buckle. The cold winter winds off the harbor would make her shiver when we went for our walks. Now she could be as warm as her mistress.

One Christmas season, when Bootsie was almost two years old, a great event took place in both our lives. My father was going to pick up some merchandise from our furniture warehouse in the commercial part of town. I asked to go along, as it always intrigued me to wander through the aisles of cartons. Bootsie jumped in the car alongside of me and off we went. An hour passed and my father had completed his business. It was time to return, but we couldn't find Bootsie. She didn't respond to my anxious call and no matter where we looked she was nowhere to be found. It was closing time. The street lights came on and most reluctantly, we had to leave.

"Don't worry," my father said assuredly. "We'll come back tomorrow and Bootsie will be here."

For five days we searched the neighborhood surrounding the warehouse, letting everyone know of my loss. In the beginning, I cried every day and wouldn't even eat my favorite foods. But one night I began to pray, not just for her return, but that wherever she was someone was caring for her and that she was safe. I knew God would answer my prayers as He always did — just like when I prayed for Joe Louis to win over Max Schmelling. For some reason, I thought at the time, this was important enough for my sincere intervention. Christmas eve arrived and no Bootsie. That night I prayed as fervently as a nine year old could, making as many deals with my Maker as I thought reasonable, and at last fell asleep peacefully.

Very early on Christmas morning, I was awakened by the

phone ringing. I could hear my mother saying, "Thank you. They'll be right there." "Hurry up, Jeanie," she said excitedly, "Dad has gone to get the car so you can go to the warehouse. He'll tell you all about it on the way."

"A fire broke out during the night in the store next door," he explained, "And when the owners arrived after the fire department called, they saw a little brown dog huddled in our doorway. Wasn't that lucky they were there to call us?"

We pulled up in front of the building. I dashed inside. In moments, Bootsie was in my arms. As she licked away my tears, I could feel her warm, full tummy. Buckling her coat, it was clear she had been bathed and been taken care of very well.

When I got home, the rest of the family were waiting to open our presents. I never did get around to my stocking that year. Nothing seemed important, not even my new baby doll and cradle, as no gift could compare to the joy I was feeling. As I was happily playing with Bootsie, it occurred to my child-thought that even though she must have spent the last week with a family who had given her food and shelter, my little dog was ready to risk cold and uncertainty to find her way back because she loved me most. My prayers had indeed been answered that Christmas morn and my best friend was home again with me.

Chapter 8
VINNIE FAVADA TALKS RELIGION

Alfred Johansen, my ten-year-old boyfriend, would ring the doorbell to see if I could come out and play. His younger brother, Walter, was at his side, as usual, as lots of kids were responsible for their siblings. Yes, I'd be right down as soon as I got some chalk and a skate key.

I'd round up Sylvia Ducker and the four of us would be ready for an afternoon of fun on the street. First we'd draw lines and boxes to play potsy (or hopscotch, as it is called in other parts of the world). We'd use the skate key to toss into the boxes, and depending on how crowded the street would become, we'd stay at it until someone suggested we move on.

This was not a favorite game for boys. They preferred "buck, buck, how many fingers are up?" One player had to bend over facing a wall, holding tightly to his knees, and one by one we'd jump onto his back and call out "buck, buck" putting up as many fingers as we desired. The bent over one had to guess correctly or he'd stay put until he came up with the right answer or his back wore out.

One day, near the end of the school year, we were playing on the stoops of the cold-water flats, when suddenly I was hit between the shoulders with a hard rubber ball. It came from across the street where several boys were playing stickball.

My friends surrounded me, as I was visibly winded, and when I caught my breath, I saw a boy approaching the curb. He swept off his cap and bowed mockingly saying, "Jeez, I'm sorry. I hope I dint hurt cha." Standing there smiling was a boy about twelve years old, with straight black hair falling over speckled green eyes. He had on wrinkled cotton knickers and knee socks hanging over scuffed shoes.

"I'm Vinnie Favada and yeah, I know who you are. You're Mr. Brown's kid. Now that ya got my 'pology, can ya give me back da ball? Da guys are waitin' for me."

Unknowingly, I had been clutching the ball in my sweaty hands and I quickly returned it to him. As he started for the street, he turned: "Say, why dontcha come across some day and I'll give ya a ride on my new bike. Ya know, to make up for hittin' ya? See ya!"

There was something about Vinnie that thoroughly charmed me, so much so as to make me want to violate the cardinal rule about crossing the street just to be with him. I knew the odds of my being caught were pretty good. But it sure was worth the excitement I felt the first time I shyly entered Vinnie's realm and declared I was ready to take the promised bike ride.

"Glad to see ya," he said, not at all surprised. "I'll hold da bike steady while ya hop on da bar."

I was apprehensive, as I had never done anything quite so daring. From the second step of the stoop, I managed to position myself side-saddle on the cross bar, grab on to the left handle and hold on to Vinnie's right arm. We were off like the wind towards 4th Avenue, separating pedestrians as we flew by. Round the corner we went, and I couldn't find my voice to tell him I definitely did not want to go down Ovington Avenue. But my fate was sealed. I could barely see the sloping hill through my scrunched-up eyes, but here we were zooming past the hospital where I was born and, I was convinced that it was here I was going to die.

Vinnie finally applied the brakes as he slowly gained on 5th Avenue, and I came back to life. He was laughing as he pedaled towards his house.

"Howze dat for a ride? Thought ya weren't gonna make it, huh? Next time, we'll go over to da park."

I don't think there'll be a next time, I told myself, as I tried to get my wobbly legs to carry me across the trolley tracks back home before I was missed.

Now that I knew adventure awaited me if I sought out Vinnie, I was eager to see more of him.

"I'm going to take a picnic lunch to the park with Sylvia," I told my mother one Saturday as I was making sandwiches. But I was meeting Vinnie at the corner and we were going to spend the afternoon on the Staten Island Ferry. The terminal was several long blocks away at the foot of our street. For a nickel we could ride all day between Bay Ridge and Staten Island if we didn't get off the ferry. We sat on the top deck eating the sandwiches I brought, watching the seagulls dive after the tugboats. An ocean liner passed, leaving huge swells behind, and rocked us like a toy sailboat. A barge went by laden with containers at one end and laundry flapping in the breeze at the other. We'd wave, make faces and yell silly things to anyone on board, knowing they could never retaliate.

Later we went down to the lower deck to hear the accordion player sing his old Italian love songs. We made sure to be home by 4 o'clock so no one would be suspicious.

There was just one more Saturday left before I went away for the summer, so we wanted to plan a fitting, final rendezvous.

"Next Saday, let's go to Coney, to Steeplechase Park," Vinnie suggested.

"I don't know. That's pretty far away and it'll cost too much. Besides, I could really get in trouble this time," I cautioned.

"Well, all ya need is sevendy fi cents — fi cents each way on da subway; fiddy cents to get in, includin' all da rides; fi cents for a hot dog, tree cents an orange drink, and I'll buy ya ices, so you'll even have money left over."

It would be at least two months before I could see Vinnie again, and I hadn't been discovered yet, so why not take the risk?

"Okay," I agreed. "I'll have to break open my piggy bank and there's always some coins in the cushions of my father's chair. Ten o'clock next week at the subway."

I was getting pretty good at making up stories by now, so when I asked my mother if I could join some girls from school to go to Steeplechase Park, she not only said "yes" but gave me fifty cents plus carfare. When I kissed her goodbye, boy, did I feel rotten.

Vinnie was waiting for me at the subway entrance. He had put on a Sunday suit and his black hair was slicked back. I looked nice, too, in a hand embroidered blouse from Hungary and my best skirt. I wished I could wear long pants like the boys, since it was difficult to maintain a lady's decorum going on those rides.

The salt air greeted us with a rush as we made our way from the station to Surf Avenue. All I remember from that point on was that it was a day of perpetual motion. From the steeplechase horses on their steel tracks, through the rotating barrels, down the slippery slides onto the turntables, the loop-de-loop, the merry- go-round and the suicide bump cars. I could hardly swallow my Nathan's hot dog and steaming sauerkraut. I was very quiet on the ride home, feeling fortunate that even though the subway cars lurched, at least they were going in a straight line.

Vinnie and I said our goodbyes without so much as a handshake. We knew we were good friends and we'd meet again when summer was over.

Actually, I didn't see Vinnie until October. I was very busy with my new school term, buying clothes and supplies for class.

Late one afternoon, I was coming home from the library when I walked right into Vinnie Favada.

"Watcha tryin' to do — get even wid me?" he jested. "I've been lookin' for ya, but ya never around."

I explained I had been busy, but I was really glad to see him. He looked shorter than I remembered, and something was decidedly different.

"Hey, my brudda Joseph has dis new car, and I'm supposed ta watch it for him while he's having supper. Ya could sit in da back seat wid me and we can talk."

"All right, but I have to be home by six."

We sat on the scratchy, brown, mohair seats of his brother's model A Ford. Vinnie proudly said Joseph was given this car because he had an important job as runner for the Syndicate. "I help Joseph polish it and my job is to keep da kids from sittin' on da fenders or gettin' their fingers all over da windas."

"Now, Jeanie, I got something to tell ya dats really important," he said. This was the only time he called me Jeanie. It was always, "Kid" or "Girl".

"Dis summer I became an altar boy at St. Dominick's," he began. "I've already served my foist mass. See, I had to get a haircut and got to keep my fingernails clean. My mudda's real happy, but she won't let me run around so much no more."

I looked at his face. His green eyes were somber and serious.

"Ya know, I really like you, Jeanie, but I can't never be ya boyfriend. Ya don't go to confession and ya not part a da church. Remember once I toll ya about ya soul? How your born wid it nice and clean, but every time ya do somethin' bad, ya get a black mark on it?"

How well I remembered that! I pictured my soul as a starched, white hankie residing in the area of my appendix, and by now undoubtedly Xed out with my transgressions.

"Ya see, my soul is as white as snow 'cause I go to confession — say a few Our Faddas and seven Hail Mary's, and I got nuthin to worry about."

At this point, to my amazement, Vinnie unbuttoned his shirt. Before my eyes I could see a row of silver medals pinned to his ribbed underwear.

"Dis is St. Rosalia, martyred saint of Palermo in Sicily, where my family comes from; dis one is St. Rocco, he protected people from the bubonic plague," Vinnie carefully explained, pointing each one out. "Here's St. Christopher — he keeps me from being lost, and dis one is St. Anthony, my patron saint. And den, of course, dere's da Virgin Mother and Our Lord on da cross."

I was impressed!

"And what's in that little bag?" I asked, noticing a sack hanging from a cord around his neck.

"Oh, dat's garlic and camphor so I don't catch cold. Ya see, some day da world is comin' to an end in a ball of fire, and I'm sorry you're gonna end up in hell. So, I gotta find myself an Italian girl or maybe become a priest."

Now for the second time, I crossed the trolley tracks on wobbly legs. This time it was even more horrific than the bike ride. I could hardly wait to get home to make a full confession to my mother in hopes of cleaning up the mess on my soul.

I prayed every night on bended knee, even after my mother and I had already said our evening prayers together. And it was at least a year before a brilliant sunset again became a thing of beauty and not a warning that my end was imminent.

Chapter 9
TARPAPER DREAMS

My kitchen window served as a passageway to adventure. Just as Alice went down the rabbit hole, I could climb over the rough, concrete sill onto the deck-like roof and be transformed. The gravel and tarpaper extended to the backyards of the stores below and connected with seven other flats. This created easy access to each neighbor, so an unwritten law of privacy existed. Being on the roof was confined to your own area and definitely no running! Every footfall could be heard by my father in our furniture store, so I fairly floated over the sticky surface on those days I chose to make the roof my playing field rather than the city streets.

On hot summer nights, my mother would carry out a couple of collapsible canvas beach chairs. She'd position them so we could catch the slightest breeze coming off the Narrows Harbor several blocks away. Then, in what were rare moments of stillness, she would open up the heavens to me. "See, there's the Big Dipper, and over there is Orion the Hunter with his sword."

Before long I could point out the Milky Way and the Pleiades or Seven Sisters. Sometimes, when my father closed the store early, the family would have ice cream under the stars. My grandmother, who lived right next door, would often join us.

Not long after Grandma moved here from Manhattan to be near my mother, a door to replace her kitchen window was installed. She spread an old oriental rug over the tarpaper. With a few potted plants around you could hardly notice the string mop and galvanized bucket in the corner. Most Sunday afternoons at four she would entertain her Hungarian clan royally, serving tea and spritz cookies.

Reading books and daydreaming were my favorite pastimes to do on the roof. I'd read at least a book a week and memorize several pages of poetry. When my father enlarged the store, he built an extension covering two backyards and expanded my viewing territory to 68th Street. Now I could peer into other yards to see how people lived around the corner. I thought I might even make a new friend.

Often after a Saturday matinee at the Alpine Movie Theater, it was de rigueur to retire to the extension with a playmate and review as closely as possible the entire scenario. I particularly loved the musicals. Being Dick Powell or Ruby Keeler was the ultimate. However, my terpsichorean efforts were always short lived. An urgent message would come from below to my mother. "For Chrissakes, get her off the roof before it collapses."

Near the end of prohibition, my father decided to build what he called a "penthouse" for me. This was his way to keep his eight-year-old daughter off the street. Two doors away there was a boarded-up, but active speakeasy, and unruly drunks sometimes interrupted the games we were playing. And on the days "Dutch" Schultz and his thugs supervised the delivery of bootleg barrels of beer, it was best not to be around.

There was also an underlying reason (of which I was totally unaware at the time) as my father had received a threatening kidnap note that put my life in peril. The note stated, "If you want to keep your little girl, place $5,000 in small bills in a valise and leave it behind the billboard on 67th Street." The note went on to give further instructions. At this point, the FBI was called in. For one month I wondered why I was being followed to school by two strange looking men in gray fedora hats driving a black sedan. I guess they scared off the perpetrators, as nothing happened.

The construction of the playhouse took six weeks and three days, but it seemed like forever to me. I observed the placement of every two-by-four and penny nail. At its completion, even I was amazed at its dimensions. My father seemed to have been carried away with his own idea, and what was to be a simple playhouse was indeed a penthouse. It was the size of a normal room, large enough to hold a 9"x12" linoleum floor covering. It had a pitched roof, six sashed windows and a double Dutch door. There was electricity, but no heat.

I couldn't wait to make it mine. For about a week I had exclusive rights moving in my dolls, games and assorted treasures. My mother put up organdy curtains, which I thought was just fine, as it was beginning to look like Heidi's cabin in the mountains. But, gradually, cartons of merchandise were moved in so surreptitiously that it took about a year for me to realize it was no longer exclusively mine.

Late one October, around my tenth birthday, my father made wine from black concord grapes. I remember it well as the kitchen stove, floor and bathtub never really got over that hue. He strained all the grapes with cheesecloth and funneled the juice into long necked bottles and stored them in my penthouse on the roof.

It was on a Saturday night, a few weeks later after an early frost had set in. We were suddenly awakened by sounds as if the Mafia were shooting up the speakeasy. But it was only the wine bottles exploding one by one all over my playhouse.

I lost interest in the roof when my hideaway became a warehouse. But by then I was going to summer camp and doing my daydreaming elsewhere.

Chapter 10
WHAT A BEAUTIFUL DAY
FOR A SUNDAY OUTING

After the demise of our old, moldy Buick, my father purchased a 1933 LaSalle. Now there was a car! I recall this elegant automobile with much pride and affection. It had grace and beauty unsurpassed by any of the other cars on the road.

Our LaSalle was used only on Sundays and was kept under a canvas cloth in a commercial garage all week to keep the dust off the finish. It was dove gray and matched my father's spats. It had double doors that opened from the middle and two crystal bud vases on each side of the windows. Adorning the hood was a polished chrome winged lady. And when I stepped onto the running board and made my way across the upholstered seats, I felt I was in Cinderella's coach.

Since my parents worked six days a week, Sunday was declared "family day" and no part of it was to be wasted in church. On those special days when we were spared a collection run, my father would walk to the corner garage, make sure there was plenty of gas and drive the LaSalle up in front of the house. This would give my mother about twenty minutes to put the dishes in the sink, throw a spread over the beds, dress two children and be downstairs before my father would lean on the horn.

My brother would sit in the front with my father and I in the back with my mother — a peaceful solution to unrestricted horseplay. Off we would go in our Sunday splendor to Uncle Charlie's in Coney Island or Uncle Ernest's in the Bronx. Other surprises awaited us according to my father's whims.

He would ride the accelerator like an organist pumping away at a Bach prelude and, with his Corona Corona already lighted, and with the smoke bellowing towards the back, you could be sure I was just a half hour away from being carsick.

Visiting relatives was my least favorite way to spend the day. However, when we drove up to my Aunt Esther's and Uncle Ernest's two story Victorian that they shared with her widowed sister, Sadie, and two sons, I was actually glad to be there. It was a storybook house with a veranda and wicker rockers. There was an attic at the top of the third landing and a wide banister that was perfect for sliding down. My aunt, uncle and cousin Gladys lived upstairs and Sadie lived downstairs and did most of the cooking.

The two families and guests ate in the commodious, paneled dining room, being offered the best dishes of the two sisters. What I really liked most was the feeling there was a lot of love in that house. Everyone talked quietly and respectfully to each other.

At least once a month we'd go to an ethnic restaurant. Sometimes it would be in Chinatown, Germantown, or Little Italy in Greenwich Village. We didn't go to Hungarian restaurants too often, as my father liked my mother's cooking better. Mostly, we'd end up at Howard Johnson's or Child's. A treat could be the Automat where the food didn't count as much as the fun of putting the nickels into the slots. I was a terrible eater with "eyes bigger than my stomach" and I'd get scolded for not finishing my food. Polite people didn't take leftovers home, and of course there were starving children in Armenia that were being deprived of nourishment because I didn't finish my mashed potatoes.

One Thanksgiving, after a particularly busy time at the store, my mother rebelled and refused to cook the holiday dinner. My father had just the solution and in retrospect, it surely was a reprimand to my mother. He took us all, including my sister home from Cornell and Grandma, to a vegetarian restaurant in Manhattan. It was a dreadful affair — sawdust-type "turkey" patties and camouflaged everything else. "Eat it, it's good for you!" he said, and to prove a point, he cleaned his plate.

The awful silence in the car going home that night was broken only by my mother, softly sobbing on my grandmother's shoulder.

Other excursions were much more pleasant. I loved the trips to the Prospect Zoo and the nearby Botanical Gardens. An afternoon like that might end up at a fishing pier in Sheepshead Bay for dinner.

Since my brother and I were too young to see vaudeville shows, my father thought we were ready for opera. Just as he insisted that Thanksgiving, "Eat it, it's good for you," he felt the same way about music. "Listen, it's good for you!"

Eight or nine year olds are not made for four and a half hours of "Othello." It was performed at the old Hippodrome, which had bleacher seats but no popcorn or hot dogs. What a relief it was to see most of the cast dying, as I knew it must be near the end of the performance and I would be free again. "Aida" wasn't so bad, as they did have real elephants whose deposits required cleaning up after each scene.

Then there was Billy Rose's "Jumbo," also at the Hippodrome and no doubt using some of the same elephants left over from "Aida." That was my first view of a live Broadway production and I could actually understand what was going on. I was awestruck.

After the enchantment of those performances wore off, the routine of a series of uninterrupted visits to relatives set in. I found I just couldn't face another Sunday.

"I'm not going with you today!" I uttered this powerful statement of emancipation when I was twelve years old. My argument was that my brother had already taken this step a few times (using the pretense of homework) and I didn't see why I couldn't be afforded the same consideration. "I'm old enough to take care of myself," I said confidently.

Reluctantly, my parents acquiesced with the provision I stay around the house and not take off on my own. Seeing my parents and brother drive off gave me a surge of fierce independence. At last, I'd have a whole day to myself to do as I pleased.

I decided to settle myself on the lounge in my parents' bedroom. It had good light from the airshaft and I could spread myself out comfortably. First, I finished my homework, to get it out of the way.

I picked up Edgar Allen Poe's *Tales of Mystery and Imagination* as a challenge and started to read, "Murders in the Rue Morgue." Very soon, I decided that was too scary to handle on a day alone, so I finished the last chapters of *The Scarlet Letter* that I had been reading. That provided me with a few minutes of a good cry.

Next on my agenda was the examination of several shoeboxes of samples. Anytime I found a coupon, I sent away for the product — anything from cereal to deodorant, it didn't matter. I never used any of it but at least I was assured of a steady flow of mail.

About 12:30, I was getting hungry, so I fixed myself a sardine sandwich and a bowl of tomato soup. I couldn't believe only two hours had passed since my family had gone, and that left five more hours of freedom.

"Now, what am I going to do?" I thought, getting a bit apprehensive.

I picked up the phone and called two friends, but one wasn't in and the other had company. There's always the picture show, but it was no fun going by myself. Everything was closed, even the ice cream parlor.

I moved my stuff into the front room so I could look out into the street. Even the trolley cars were slow in coming by. Looking each way, I could see none of my street friends were around either.

In desperation, I said, "O.K., Bootsie, I'll take you for a walk." At least, I'd make someone happy.

We went to the park and I sat on a bench watching a few people walk by. One person actually asked what breed of a dog I had, possibly to embarrass me. On the way back home, I heard a heavenly sound of melodious chimes. The Good Humor truck just turned down the street. I bought a chocolate covered popsicle and shared it with Bootsie. "You're the only friend I have today."

As it was getting dark and I was becoming anxious, I saw the car drive up and Mother and Laurie step out.

I never was so overjoyed to see anyone, but I wasn't going to let them know. When they came up the stairs, I was absorbed in a book and barely paid any notice.

"Did you have a good day?" Mother asked as she kissed me. "Just fine," I lied.

"We went to Aunt Peggy's and she took us to the SeaFare for lobster thermidor," my brother taunted.

Well, you can be sure the next week I was first downstairs into the car all ready and waiting for the Bach prelude to begin, as we all embarked on another Sunday outing.

Chapter 11
LOOK OUT FOR THE SWINGING DOOR

When my grandmother, who lived next door, died in 1935, we broke through the wall between the two apartments. With some major renovations, we ended up with eight rooms and two baths, an unheard of arrangement for the era, especially if you lived on 69th Street.

My father had more than luxury in mind as his plan was to create a living showroom. He started with the kitchen, taking away my mother's beloved gas stove and replacing it with the first Westinghouse electric range. Linoleum was torn up and white vinyl squares lay in its place. Built in cabinets with a working counter of metal covered one wall. Even the sink was enclosed in a metal cabinet. All was to be strictly modern, except my mother refused to give up her gas refrigerator which stood like a monolith on its tall legs. She bought some paint to freshen its appearance, but the result looked like scabs hanging on the door and the gasket forever stuck each time we opened or closed it.

Our morning routine would see my father and mother arising at 8 a.m. While breakfast was being prepared, my father went downstairs to sweep the entry and sidewalk in front of the store. It was at this time, I'd grab my orange juice and cup of Postum so I'd be on my way to school before the daily onslaught began. At 8:30 sharp, the freshly squeezed orange juice, not a single seed, please, strained into a water glass; two 3 minute eggs, twice burnt toast and strong perked coffee served with the thick skim of scalded milk, would be waiting on the table. Everything had to be served exactly to my father's wishes or the air would be ringing with epithets. My father never cussed beyond "hell" and "damn," but he made ample and emphatic use of them.

All our meals except for holidays took place in the breakfast room, the prettiest room in the house, I thought. The wallpaper had a charcoal gray background with strawberry bunches on a vine. The dinette set, of bleached maple made by Heywood Wakefield, came with a china closet and server in art deco lines. My grandmother's settee, bought from an auction at the Waldorf Astoria, sat in front of the window overlooking the airshaft that separated the two apartments.

We had two bathrooms, one in the original white hexagonal tile and claw footed bathtub and the other, next to my parents' room, had been redone in rose-colored tile including all the fixtures.

Our dining room was Spanish Conquistador style, to appeal to the Italian customers, with all pieces in dark mahogany. The massive table with elephantine legs could seat ten people on its cut velvet high back chairs. There was a buffet, china closet and server that sat on an oriental rug. A liquor cabinet, with the heads of Columbus and Queen Isabella, stood in one corner. Over the server, which doubled as my toy box, was an oil painting of two stags in the woods.

Discriminating clients could choose from items in the living room, truly a work of art. You entered through an archway from the dining room onto wall-to-wall broadloom carpet, a new innovation for the time. White on white embossed satin wallpaper covered the walls. A closet that was part of a former bedroom became a built-in bar and radio with lighted blue mirror backing. I was credited with this addition as I had seen one just like it in a movie.

I remember the day the nine foot royal blue, velvet sofa with the cream colored fringe was delivered. Coming home from school, I saw this monstrous piece being hoisted through an upstairs window. I gasped in horror as I thought someone had surely died. Wasn't that a coffin being shoved through the window? The other pieces in the room were a gentleman's chair of garnet velvet with cream leather arms, matching ottoman, and a lady's high back chair covered in gold damask. Three walnut tables had smoky blue mirrors for tops. A baby grand piano, where my mother practiced Chopin etudes daily, filled one corner. Sheet music from current musicals and operettas were in the bench, always available when my father honored us with a recital. A copy of Breughel's *Harvest* hung over a low bookcase. My mother took art classes at the New School, in Greenwich Village, and minutely copied the Breughel. She later hung her copy in its place. Now, we had an original.

In order to get to the other part of the house, we had to go through a set of swinging doors into a large room that never had a purpose. There was a cot, for when my sister came home from school, shelves for books, a walk-in closet and the rest of the space, so it wouldn't be a total loss, was filled with cartons of merchandise. If a pathway hadn't been left open, my brother and I could not have gotten to our rooms.

My room faced the street. I was allowed to choose a four-poster, walnut bed and dresser to match, and after much persuasion, got a kidney shaped dressing table and three-way mirror. I could sit in front of this mirror and become my own worst critic. Freckles, why so many of them? Braces, when will they ever come off? Is that a blackhead I see? Perhaps I should start tweezing my eyebrows? Only forty more strokes of the hairbrush and then I can go to bed. My brother would tease me with what he thought was endless scrutiny of a hopeless situation.

The main attraction in my brother's room was a Simmons vibrator bed. We were warned not to use it as it might wear out before my father's need to demonstrate it elapsed. We put it to the test for ourselves and friends and couldn't find anything worth getting into trouble over.

A complete maple suite occupied my parents' bedroom. It was large enough for twin beds, two dressers and a chaise lounge. The hallway outside the bedroom was the covered stairwell from our original apartment. With the high skylight, it made a perfect location for the Singer sewing machine. While my mother wasn't a great seamstress, she could create miracles out of crepe paper. All my costumes for grade school plays, from a yellow chickadee to Little Red Riding Hood, she turned out on this machine. I won first place in a contest representing the Baker's Chocolate girl all dressed in yards of brown paper.

Several times a week, at least the first year of the renovation, my father would buzz upstairs and urgently command, "Get the dishes out of the sink and Bootsie on the roof. I'm bringing someone up to see the kitchen," or "Tell Mother I want to show the master bedroom."

Fortunately, nothing was ever sold off the floor. We could keep what we had. Living in a showroom gave me the feeling that nothing was permanent, and best not to get attached to objects. When I stopped playing with a particular toy or ceased reading one of my books, or outgrew any of my clothes — off they went to younger cousins. Nothing seemed to come in my direction, however.

I was proud to live in the latest fashion, but I would have traded it in a minute for a little house with a tree in front and a small closet filled with old, favorite things.

Chapter 12
GIVE US THIS DAY OUR DAILY NEWSPAPER

In the 1930s, women newspaper writers were called "sob sisters." My older sister, Violet, 10 years my senior, was one of them. She graduated cum laude in Journalism with a Phi Beta Kappa key from Cornell University. Despite the Depression and the fact that she was a girl, Vi miraculously was hired by the prestigious *Brooklyn Eagle,* a paper in existence since 1841. After a stint as a columnist in the hinterlands of Long Island, my 21-year-old sheltered sister became a street reporter. She'd come home with tales of speakeasy raids, waterfront murders and cats caught up telephone poles. I'd listen fascinated with these tales, wishing for the day I could do the same.

She also did book reviews and was able to keep the copies that would end up in our bookcase. Somehow, I instinctively knew the books, which would be deemed unsuitable for my eyes. And to this day, I can't forget the world I discovered when I read and reread *The Postman Always Rings Twice.* It was on the shelf next to my treasured *Japanese Fairy Tales.*

Our relationship was not what you'd call sisterly the times I remember her home. Vi left for college on a scholarship at the age of 16, and I was just entering grade school. She was like a second mother, but one who gave me her undivided attention. All the children's books I acquired, from *Hans Brinker, or The Silver Skates* to poetry anthologies were gifts from her. Vi would take me on outings to museums in Manhattan, and we'd play that I was her little girl. I still have a few letters from first and second grade, one in which I wrote, "Dear Violet, How are you feeling? How is your tooth? I am a good girl. Things are going on very nisely," Jean Brown, October 17, 1931.

She also protected me from the onslaughts of our brother, Laurie. He, of the velvet eyes and curly dark hair, the off- the-scale I.Q. that caused him to immerse himself in music and math before I was into my multiplication tables, was forever getting me in trouble. Vi saw that it was really he who started each ruckus by punching me in the stomach. I'd run screaming to my mother, who in a most unperturbed way would accuse me of being the instigator by disturbing Laurie's studies. Vi would comfort me and tell him to back off.

It was evident that I adored her, so when she asked if I would help the cause by stuffing envelopes during the *Brooklyn Eagle* strike, I was more than willing to do so.

This was the longest and most bitter newspaper strike ever to hit the New York area. Members of the Newspaper Guild were staff writers who were striking to gain the same prestige, salary and security as other professions. At age 12, I had my first experience of a labor / management dispute.

One Saturday, I was working at headquarters, a prison type building with bars on the windows, when a call came in for a volunteer to hand out leaflets at Abraham and Strauss, the largest department store in Brooklyn. A. & S. was continuing its advertising despite the union's efforts asking for their support. I was to distribute flyers requesting shoppers not to patronize that establishment. I looked nothing like a flaming radical, wearing my Scotch plaid skirt and my royal velvet Glengarry bonnet. Yet, I wasn't at my post for more than ten minutes when a woman pushed me aside and said to her companion, "Don't take nothing from that communist kid." In no time I was back at headquarters stuffing envelopes.

That Christmas, the strikers' children were treated to a party. There was entertainment and small gifts. But the most excitement was when a beefy looking man with a face like a mastiff handed out personalized autographed baseballs. It was Babe Ruth.

Violet's gift to me was a pair of black fishnet stockings and a red felt carnation. I was surprised and perplexed when I opened the box. I didn't question her, as I knew the strike had depleted her funds. Undoubtedly, it was passed down from a grab bag and had little significance. But I felt she had sent a message to me: Dare to be different, Little Sister!

Chapter 13
SCHOOL DAYS WALKABOUT

"Neither Snow, nor Rain, nor Gloom of Night Stays These Couriers from the Swift Completion of Their Appointed Rounds" is emblazoned on the New York Post Office to honor the stalwart men who daily defy the elements so the mail will be delivered. But there was no such sign on Public School 170 to honor the intrepid six to thirteen year olds who every day had to make two round trips to further their education.

For nine years, starting with kindergarten, I trod the same path. My mother escorted me the first year, on a very short rein, dropping me off at 9:00 a.m. and retrieving me at 11:30. I had two busy commercial intersections to cross and two residential streets. I was instructed to "Cross at the corners and look both ways, and you will be safe for the rest of your days." Life was simple: red meant "stop" and green meant "go" — no yellow caution light to give me a chance to go for it. I learned how many minutes it should take from the time I left home until I got to the classroom. Average time for little legs was twenty minutes. I didn't own a watch nor could I tell time, but that first year my mother made it plain, "Jeanie, you can't dawdle anywhere along the route or you'll be late and you know, late has its consequences."

From the time I was six, in first grade, I was on my own, although my brother was supposed to keep an eye on me. We'd be launched from home at the same time, but that would be the last contact until he'd show up at the corner of our block to make sure we'd get home together.

We couldn't bring our lunch as there was no cafeteria, and kids were not allowed in the schoolyard unsupervised. So, at 11:30, we would be sent home, stomachs growling. I'd have to bolt down lunch in fifteen minutes in order to get back to school before the bell rang. This was when I began to wish I were poor. Then, I could stay in a warm classroom and have hot tomato soup and white bread. And, if I only lived a half block to the west, I would have been in a different school district and not have to walk so far.

I remember each step of the way. No matter the weather and type of clothing, pounds of outerwear or a summer frock, there was always the ever-present school bag crammed with a pencil box, ruler and textbooks and unrelated items to weigh me down.

My itinerary carried me past the laundry, the boarded-up speakeasy with movie posters plastered on it, the candy store, the tailor shop and my favorite diversion, the tropical fish store. All of these establishments were frequent stops after school where I'd visit with merchants — except of course, the speakeasy. Then, I'd come to an apartment house, some more row houses and the florist. For five cents, the florist would sell me a bouquet of flowers from the gleanings of wedding and funeral arrangements. I'd do this for my mother on every holiday that was marked in red on the calendar. Next to the florist was the shoemaker, a kindly, old man who looked, to me, like Geppetto. Passing the barbershop still made me cringe. One spring, my mother had Mr. Antonelli cut off my bangs and give me a stylish boyish bob. I hid in my room and wouldn't come out for days. On the corner was the cigar store where I'd purchase my father's Cuban Corona Coronas for a quarter. He'd give me the silver cylinders they came in and I'd use the colored bands for rings.

I remember getting ready to cross the street, sometimes waiting for two lights to change just to make sure it was safe. I'd leap onto the sidewalk on the other side to find myself at Ebinger's window. I'd have just enough time in the bakery to buy myself a cupcake to eat on the way. The stores that lined the avenue were where my mother shopped. There was the grocer, the fruit market, the pork store with the pig's head on ice in the window, and the fresh poultry store, reeking so badly it covered the odors of the nearby fish market.

Here, I crossed the avenue and above the stationery store was Carbrey's Dancing School. On Saturday mornings, I'd climb the stairs to the studio for lessons. I had my 50 cents tied tightly in a handkerchief, stuffed in the pocket of my rompers. Mrs. Carbrey, a heavily made-up lady with a powder-caked face and heavy eyelashes, played the piano. Mr. Carbrey, a silver-haired man sporting a leather bow tie, taught tap and acrobatics. I can still hear the pennies clinking in my taps as I times-stepped on the bamboo-slotted mat. For two years I aspired to become my idol, Ruby Keeler, but all the solos at the recitals at the Knights of Columbus were given to the double-jointed kids who could end their numbers with cartwheels and splits. The chorus line was not where I wanted to be.

The best part of my walk was now approaching. From the noisy avenue, I was entering a street of tidy homes, miniature lawns and climbing roses. Chestnut and elm trees lined each side forming an arbor. On sunny days, the sidewalk was dappled with rays like an impressionist painting. I'd play "step on a crack and you'll break your mother's back," never once stepping outside the line. Certain times of the year, there were pods from the trees that if you split open could be put on the bridge of your nose where they'd remain for the longest time.

In the winter, the snow stayed clean on this street, perfect for snowball making. But it wasn't as much fun as climbing the gray, brown mountains along the avenue.

Two more blocks and there was my school, my place of learning. In my walk, I covered six blocks one way, twenty-four blocks a day under bright skies and inclement weather, and it was fair to say I learned a lot, just from my goings and comings.

Chapter 14
FRIDAY AFTERNOON ASSEMBLY

I attended Public School 170. It was a standard copy of most of the red brick edifices of the time, with concrete steps leading to an imposing entry. That was used for the first day of school and visitors. We entered by a side door and went straight to our homerooms.

There were thirty desks with attached seats, inkwells and years of accumulated initials and dates carved with penknives. The rooms were bright and pleasant, each with a picture on the wall over the blackboard. It took me several years to discover the painting was of George Washington, the Father of our Country, and not the principal.

In the thirties, it was a rarity to have a male teacher in grade school, but I was fortunate to have two. In a way, I had a crush on both of them, for different reasons.

Mr. Seltzer, my fifth grade teacher, was the first man to make me go home and look at myself in the mirror to find a positive image. Each year a vote was taken to choose the most intelligent boy and girl and also the best looking. It never occurred to either teacher or student that this was a way to create inferiorities among the less fortunate.

The same two girls won every year since kindergarten, Jane Adams, for beauty, and Jane Anderson, for being smart. This year, however, Mr. Seltzer looked the class straight into its narrow face and said, "What about Jean Brown — for both?" I almost died on the spot! Of course, the two Janes won again, but Mr. Seltzer became a hero in my eyes.

My sixth grade teacher, Mr. Linwood, looked like a movie idol. He was tall, blond-haired, blue-eyed and had teeth like an ear of fresh white corn. I always sat up front in my classes since I was small, so I was able to do little errands for him with ease.

Sometimes, I would wait for him after school so we could walk together to the subway. I saw to it that we never failed to have things to talk about. Mr. Linwood must have been aware of a growing attachment, and the conversation soon ran to his wife and the expectancy of their first child.

This didn't stop our friendship, and one day he did introduce me to a pretty Mrs. Linwood and their new baby.

Every Friday afternoon, we had assembly for the first through sixth grades. It was here we put on our plays, sang songs, heard announcements or volunteered any of our talents.

My sister returned from college one semester with a book of tavern songs which I proceeded to memorize. A great one, I thought, was "The Man on the Flying Trapeze." I practiced all the verses at home, with gestures, and decided I'd share it with the Friday afternoon assembly.

The first stanza started out fine with "He floats through the air with the greatest of ease, that daring young man on the flying trapeze" — but somehow, when I got to the part, "she rustled her bustle (with gestures) and then without shame, said 'Maybe later, not yet!' "... I was unceremoniously yanked off the platform. It was years before I understood what all the fuss was about, but it was enough to keep me off the stage until I graduated.

Chapter 15
THE FRIEND I NEVER KNEW

Like the mythological River Styx, the street where I lived separated me from those on the other side. With the constant flow of trolley cars and trucks, it was a law that I could in no way cross over. I did manage to put pennies on the tracks and retrieve them, but that was only going out 10 feet and I could quickly return to the curb without being caught.

Our two-story brick row houses faced the three story brownstones across the way. We may never have spoken to our neighbors, but somehow we knew their names and just about everything that was going on in their lives. We knew who had a job, who went to school and where, number of children in each family, who was sick and who died. There was a lot of viewing from windows in winter and much stoop sitting in nice weather. And in the evenings, if a shade wasn't pulled, the drama continued indoors.

Directly across the street, in a first floor apartment, lived Annalise Polanski. I knew all about Annalise from my mother, but also from observing and general knowledge. She was born a year after me, a change-of-life baby, a golden gift to a worn out, gray-haired lady. Shortly after birth, her father died and left a grieving widow with two grown sons to support the family.

Annalise was brought up as a cherished, protected child. She never came outdoors except to be escorted to Catholic school by one of her brothers. I'd see her leave every morning about the same time I did. She'd be wearing a navy serge uniform during the week and on Sundays she'd be dressed in an elegant coat trimmed with white rabbit fur and hat to match, all made by her mother's skilled hands. There was no sight more beautiful than when Annalise made her first communion, looking like an angel with her long blonde, tight curls — the color of taffy.

I wanted to be her friend so badly, but Mrs. Polanski wouldn't let her cross the great divide any more than my mother would let me. So, over the years, we just observed each other, being aware of our existence but not participating.

One cold December morning when I was 11, as I opened my front door, I received a chill that had nothing to do with the weather. Across the street, on the Polanskis' door, was a funeral wreath of waxen lilies. A child had died. How often I had seen the black wreaths attached ominously to the front doors. I'd watch as relatives would arrive dressed in mourning and endure the wails of grief as the coffins were carried down the stoops. Once there was even a parade that followed a horse-drawn hearse with glass windows. I was terrified of death. Hadn't I been told many times by my street friends that my final destination was hell because I didn't go to confession?

I knew Annalise had been sick. I had seen the doctor entering her house. It was said pneumonia had claimed her young life. The day of the funeral, I stayed home from school and watched as her brothers carried out the small white coffin. I did my own special mourning, crying and praying. But I knew Annalise was surely going to heaven.

For the next few months, the shades of the Polanski house were drawn shut against the world. Then, one day, I saw Mrs. Polanski at the window, and from then on that's where she stayed. She would be there in the morning when I left for school, and there when I returned. If I were out playing, I would feel her eyes following me. When I was old enough to go to the movies at night with friends, I'd see her by the light of the street lamp.

I told my mother how strange I felt being watched all the time. She explained how difficult it must have been for Mrs. Polanski to lose Annalise and she was substituting me for the little girl she could never see grow up.

The night of my Junior Prom, I stayed out until 5 a.m. as was the prescribed schedule. The format was to double date. One boy should have a car and be old enough to drive. You'd attend the dance until midnight, go to Coney Island, then sit on the boardwalk until it was light enough to go home. So, at 5 a.m., I was saying good night to my escort, gently kissing him before I entered the house. As my friends drove off, I could see a shadowy figure at her post at the window. I stood there in the light of dawn wanting her to see how pretty I looked in my first formal. Suddenly, I felt impelled to wave. Mrs. Polanski waved back.

Chapter 16
THE NIGHT WIND'S LIPS

"Tho I might be a bit jealous,
Still I've not a thing to fear,
For even tho he kissed you,
I asked him to, my dear.

Much as I've longed to hold you,
Still there was a bar between,
With a single way remaining
To be near you while unseen.

So, I let him kiss you for me,
And he breathed a sigh unknown.
'Twas the Night Wind's lips that kissed you,
But the heart, dear, was my own."

Only a week ago, I had been trying to read these carefully printed words by the fading beam of a flashlight. There was no need to hold the red paper heart closely as I knew every line of the poem. It was the favorite of the ones I received that summer. Lights out had been called hours ago, but since that was my last night at camp, I just couldn't sleep. The symphony of country creatures at camp always seemed louder than the rhythmic sounds of the clickety-clack of the trolley cars.

Tonight, lying in my own bed, I can't sleep either. I keep remembering how secure and hidden I felt under the blankets. Now, all the wondrous happenings of those past two months are running through my mind.

That was my third summer at Camp Mt. Joy, a co-educational progressive camp high in the Catskill Mountains where the legendary Rip Van Winkle once bowled. Devotion to the arts, modern dance, drama, music, and poetry were encouraged. But, sports, other than swimming or horseback riding, were considered déclassé. Boys could play basketball and volleyball, but it had to be non-competitive.

That was the summer I became a woman. Although most of the girls in my bunk were mature, it still came as a complete shock to me when one day after swim session, there IT was. I reported to my counselor who sent me to the infirmary at once. The nurse, stiff and starched, set me down and methodically repeated the litany she had so well rehearsed. What could I do but accept the burden she put on me. At last I knew why this coming of age was called "the curse." Even so, as I left, I felt something excruciatingly mystical had happened to me.

That was the summer I sang the lead in H.M.S. Pinafore. Gilbert and Sullivan's operetta was set for August and I was cast as

Josephine despite my loud protestations that I really couldn't sing. The director had discovered that I had brought my white organdy graduation dress and deemed it perfect for the part. I had to admit that it looked appropriately Josephine, and I did get kissed by the best looking senior boy. I was mortified at having to falsetto my way through the libretto. But I developed a comedic approach and the audience loved it.

That was the summer we went on an overnight hike. After breakfast at the mess hall, we stopped at the kitchen door to select sandwiches for our outing. It was always the same — tuna fish on rye or peanut butter on whole wheat carefully wrapped in wax paper. It was put in a brown paper bag with a piece of fruit and a cookie. We packed a toothbrush, soap, washcloth and that was to be all as we were told we'd be "roughing" it.

Two counselors led our group of fifteen girls out onto a country road. Before we started they informed us of the customary procedure. Our hike was to be five miles, a 10 minute break every two miles. We would picnic halfway there and arrive at the campsite around noon. There would be nature talks, games and swimming in the creek. Late afternoon, the truck would arrive with mattresses and provisions for our cookout ... steak and potatoes to be prepared over campfires built by the staff. We would spend the night and return to camp after breakfast.

That night lying on my lumpy mattress, enveloped in the remains of the aurora borealis, I felt so at one with the universe. I knew this wasn't the way the Girl Scouts camped, but we still shared the same sky.

And that was the summer I felt loved.

Jules was the swimming counselor and a sophomore at City College. He was six feet tall, muscular and his mahogany body and straight features gave him the look of an Indian warrior. I thought spending extra time with me was just his way of being sure I'd qualify for my Red Cross certificate. Yet, at times, he would stop in the middle of a sentence and look at me deeply. I found this confusing as I couldn't imagine why he'd be interested in me . . . *he was so old.*

Then, one evening, at my dinner plate there appeared a note saying, "Jeanie Brown of 10 and 4, Wants to be somebody's squaw." (Note: In Brooklyn and the Bronx, squaw rhymes with four.)

It was signed JD.

We started seeing each other occasionally, sometimes for only a few minutes whenever we could break away from our schedules. Fraternization between campers and counselors of the opposite sex was against the rules. However, once we managed to take a walk through the piney woods in the moonlight. He talked to me of what a wonderful woman I would be someday. He filled my head with philosophy and ideas that were eons beyond my comprehension. For the rest of the summer there would be love poems at my plate — some humorous, some rapturous. I had no idea how to deal with this awakening, but it sure made me feel extraordinary.

Jules called me for a date the day after we returned home from camp, just as he promised he would. Was I ready for this? I had never been asked out before. What should I wear? How should I act? I was sorry I had said "yes," but he seemed so eager to please.

I met him at Radio City Music Hall on Saturday at noon. Fellows from the Bronx never come to Brooklyn to escort their dates. I had grown in the last couple of months, and nothing seemed to fit properly. I borrowed a blouse from my mother and wore a light blue skirt that didn't fit too well either.

When I saw Jules dressed in his city clothes, he looked just as encumbered as I felt. He took me to lunch at Child's Restaurant and ordered the Blue Plate Special for two. I was so nervous I couldn't swallow a bite. After lunch, he whisked me across 6th Avenue to the Music Hall and up the regal staircase to the reserved loge seats. All during the movie, he tried desperately to hold my hand. Didn't he know people were looking? Couldn't he see that?

After the show, he humiliated me by sliding down the elegant brass banister into the lobby. What could happen next?

We strolled to Central Park, found a shady spot under a tree and sat quietly watching the people stroll by. We couldn't think of a thing to say. Suddenly, Jules looked at his watch and said, "I'll walk you to the subway." On the way to the station, just to prove his masculinity one more time, he jumped over every trash basket without turning one on end.

The summer was over. Next week I'd be back at school. The transition down from Mt. Olympus to the caverns of the city was always arduous and depressing. Yet within me there was a strange stirring like a chrysalis. I kept thinking about how I had grown out of my clothes. But, perhaps, even now, I was beginning to grow into that wonderful woman Jules saw in me — the one the night wind's lips had kissed.

Mother Elvira with sister Margaret, 1907

Father, William Brown, Firefly Opera Company, 1912

Elvira and William at the Delicatessen, San Francisco 1914

Sunday at Sea Gate, near Coney Island: aunts, uncles and cousins -
Jeanie and Laurie in the middle - 1928

Hungarian clan gathering on the roof, Brooklyn, around 1939

Baby Jeanie - one year, six months 1925

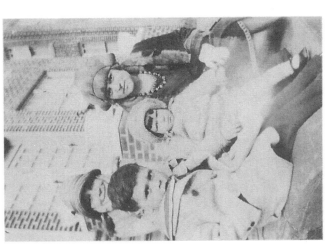

"I told you I didn't want my picture taken!" brother
Laurie, sister Violet, mother - Brooklyn, NY 1926

104

Brown Family Portrait 1931

Grandmother Julia, Brooklyn NY 1929-1935

Easter Sunday: Laurie, Alfred Johansen, Jeanie 1930

Jeanie in her Shirley Temple dress and boyish bob with brother Laurie - Roscoe, NY 1932

Dance recital at the Methodist Church
Brooklyn, NY 1933

Baker's Chocolate crepe paper costume:
Alpine Hotel, Roscoe NY, 1932

107

Grade school graduation, P.S. 170.
Dress by Mrs. Luinetti, 1938

Camp Mt. Joy, Roscoe NY, 1939

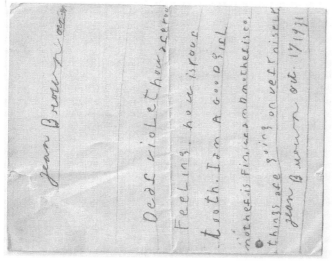

Note to sister Vi at school, 1931.

"Baby, take a bow."

Bunkmates and counselor Liz, 1940.

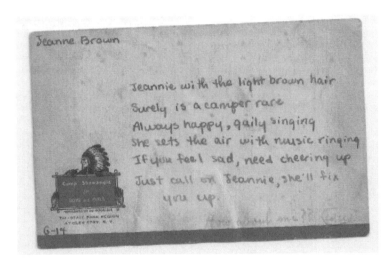

Jeanne Brown

Jeannie with the light brown hair
Surely is a camper rare
Always happy, gaily singing
She sets the air with music ringing
If you feel sad, need cheering up
Just call on Jeannie, she'll fix
you up.

"Noncompetitive and Progressive"

Part 2

JEAN

Chapter 17
SUMMER OF INNOCENCE

The summer of 1940 started out innocently enough. Being a senior at camp had certain privileges but strict adherence to the activities calendar was a must. I made my bed with perfect hospital corners, never missed lights out and could be counted on to perform all duties in an agreeable manner. But little did I know that when July was past, my orderly life would change radically.

This year I was attending Camp Shawangee, an oasis situated in the gentle foothills of the Pocono Mountains on the property of the old Singer Sewing Machine estate. Stone walls wrapped around the forty acres, making it a safe and isolated haven for boys and girls to experience camping in an elite style. Two identical large stone houses of the early twenties period were directly inside iron gates. One housed the staff while the other was used for social functions. There were many outbuildings. The dairy barn was now the mess hall and the loft, with its floor slick from years of haying, was the recreation room. Only a dirt road separated the boys' camp from the girls'.

I came to be at this exclusive camp as the modern dance counselor was daughter of friends of my parents and I had outgrown last year's camp.

Girls in my bunk were from Riverside Drive and West End Avenue, and their footlockers were full of outfits from B. Altman while mine came from a discount store in downtown Brooklyn. On top of this pauper feeling, my Dad gave me only twenty dollars spending money to last the entire two months. I was happy there but felt I couldn't continue my friendships after camp was over. Who would want to visit me on 69th Street?

On the first Saturday evening in August, I was at the lighted outdoor stage rehearsing a modern dance routine. All appeared to be going well, so we were dismissed to go to the Rec Hall where games were being held. Earlier, I had noticed a male counselor whom I had seen before on occasion, sitting on a bench watching intently. He came up to me as I was preparing to leave.

"Come on," he said in a startling persuasive manner. "Let me escort you to the hall."

A young man stood before me, more handsome than any I had ever seen. He had blue-black wavy hair, almond shaped hazel eyes and lashes that made shadows on his cheekbones. Tyrone Power, the favorite in my scrapbook, would have come in a close second.

"Get on my shoulders and I'll carry you there," he insisted. I knew he had to be at least twenty years old and I was fifteen and a half, so I figured this was a brotherly gesture. He was wearing riding britches tucked into high black leather boots. A white long sleeved shirt, open at the neck, and an aquiline nose gave him the appearance of a young Lord Byron. I hesitantly, almost hypnotically, got on his shoulders from the stage and he proceeded carefully through the cool damp grass while I held on tightly. All too soon, we could see the lights and hear the music coming from the hall.

"Go in and tell one of your friends that rehearsal is still going on and you'll see them back at the bunk. I'd like to show you something at the old barn."

I couldn't believe what was happening. Boys were frequently interested in me, but here was a grown man wanting my company. Sure, I was cute with my long, brown silky hair, roving brown eyes, smattering of freckles and turned up nose. Hadn't I come in second in a Gene Tierny contest and had my picture in the paper? But, didn't I now have braces on my teeth, a bite plate that made me talk funny sometimes and rubber bands obscuring my smile. And I wasn't yet sixteen — but maybe he didn't know that.

"Okay, I'll be right there," I answered bravely. "But, if you don't mind, let me do my own walking." We strolled away from the Rec Hall into the country darkness.

"Have you ever been to the old barn and jumped in the hayloft? It's really great, especially with the moonlight streaming through the slats."

This question was the beginning of a dilemma. On one hand I wanted to escape back to the safety of my peers, but the other urged me on to adventure and the unknown.

There was no moon that night. But we did climb the ladder to the loft and jumped into the sweet smelling haystack alongside the barn.

Afterwards, he lay with his head resting on my stomach, which nervously gurgled in unison with the crickets and bullfrogs. With a hayseed in his mouth, he proceeded to tell me that he had been planning this meeting for several weeks. He watched me ride by on Fairwind, the bay horse, and admired the way I sat in the saddle. He had observed me at the lake paddling a canoe. And, he had taken his charge of nine-year-old boys to every dance rehearsal and performance I'd been in. Yes, he knew how old I was, but he also knew I held all the potential of someone he wanted to be close to for a long time.

Then, he said poetically, "There's something so sweet and fresh about virginity. I also admire your purity."

By this time I was totally bewildered. I didn't know what to say, but nothing was needed. At this point, he got up, brushed himself off, helped me to my feet and walked me back to my bunk just in time for lights out.

"I'll see you tomorrow evening after my boys are in bed," he said matter-of-factly lighting a cigarette and then walked off quickly into the night.

Chapter 18
CUPID AND PSYCHE

The ballroom of the great, stone house was ablaze with candles. Senior campers and staff swayed to the music of the Big Bands coming through the hi-fi system. This was the last night to be together after two months of sharing each other's lives.

The girls were smartly dressed in Sunday-go-to-meeting clothes. The boys had succumbed to wearing shirts, ties and jackets — quite a contrast from the casual style they were used to.

I caught my image in the full length, baroque mirror and was startled to see how grown up I looked. I was wearing my Easter dress of lightweight wool in a lovely shade of aqua. It had long cuffed sleeves, a Peter Pan collar and double-breasted silver buttons. The cocoa brown wedgies felt comfortable as I nestled into Wes' shoulder as we danced to Frank Sinatra singing, "I'll Never Smile Again."

"From this moment, Jean, this will be our song," he said quietly as he kissed my forehead.

"Is that me?" I asked myself, still looking in the mirror as I was slowly twirled around to the rhythm of Tommy Dorsey's trombone. My long, brown hair was parted in the middle and curled under in a sweeping pageboy. I looked taller in my heels and came up to the handsome, young man's smoothly shaven chin.

Could it be it was only three weeks ago that Wes came into my life? I remember the second time we saw each other how he handed me his comb and said, "Part your hair in the middle. Pretty hair like yours should flow."

I obediently took the pins out of my pompadour and followed his directives. With that gesture, I became the object of Wes' unwavering charm and attention. It was also at this moment of metamorphosis, I became Jean. There was no place left for the girl in the rhyme my counselor, Liz, had written for our bunk picture:

Jeanie with the light brown hair
Surely is a camper rare.
Always happy, gaily singing,
She sets the air with music ringing.
If you feel sad, need cheering up,
Just call on Jeanie, she'll fix you up!

Well, this Jeanie was no longer around as I willingly, yet with trepidation, surrendered myself to Wes' blueprint for courtship.

120

He was determined to see me as often as possible, and with the help of my bunkmates, who covered for me, I was able to steal away and meet him in the clearing in the woods. In the beginning, we just talked sitting on a log, or mostly Wes did, telling of his escapades.

One afternoon, as I was working in the craft room, one of his nine year olds approached me with a note. It read, "Meet me tonight at 9 o'clock on the road to the meadow. Just bring a flashlight. I'll be waiting."

That turned out to be the most romantic night of my young life. Wes had brought a Victrola and two army blankets — one to lie on and the other to keep us warm from the cool August night.

He put on Cesar Franck's "Symphony in D Minor" and assured me that at 9:47, as the crescendo part would start, the full moon would make its appearance.

If it did as predicted, I would have to kiss him. The sounds of the orchestra filled the dark meadow. We listened in silence as we watched the fireflies dart by. I was taken in with the authoritative yet gentle way of this man, yet I wondered if I'd ever get over the disquietude it caused. He was certainly edging me to abandon my own established code of ethics.

As predicted, at precisely 9:47, a huge, orange disk started to push its way up over the tops of the pine trees. Almost in time with the music, the harvest moon emerged, flooding the meadow with amber shadows. Wes rolled over on his elbow towards me. "Time to pay off your debt." It was a sweet, impassionate kiss, more like a greeting than a homecoming. I kept trying to brush away what seemed like spider webs from my eyes but soon discovered it was Wes' amazing eyelashes caressing my cheekbones.

There were many more surprises in the next few weeks, not only for me but, for my parents. They showed up on visitors' day towards evening to see their daughter, but I was nowhere to be found. The entire camp was to be at a campfire sing-along, but Wes had planned a private campfire for the two of us. I didn't know my parents were coming, but by the time I showed up for lights out, they had returned to their motel, but not without having spoken to the Director.

What followed were reprimands from my irritated parents and warnings from my counselor. "Not only are you breaking the rules," Liz reminded me as we sat face to face on our cots, "But Wes has a reputation for having dated every female counselor so far this summer. And he just wants to add you to his conquests. Besides, he'll never see you again after camp!"

These admonitions came back to me as we joined hands singing "Auld Lang Syne" and saying our tearful goodbyes with promises to stay in touch throughout the year. Wes held me tight and promised that this was just the beginning for us. He then presented me with a beautifully hand carved letter opener made out of cherry wood with our initials entwined in a heart.

I didn't hear from Wes for two days after my return home, much to the relief of my parents. I was starting to believe what Liz had said was true.

Late that night I heard crackling noises at my bedroom window but dismissed it as the wind rattling the Venetian blinds. The next morning there was a call from Wes. "Did you hear the pennies I tossed at your window last night? It's a good thing I had a pocketful as I didn't know which one was yours."

"You mean you saw where I lived and you're still calling me?" I asked in disbelief. "Why should I care where you live when it's only you I care about?"

These magical words stirred my heart. I felt like the joyous Psyche from my mythology book when she and the beautiful winged Cupid, after many trials, had found each other at last.

Chapter 19
THE SWEETEST DAY OF ALL

The big day had arrived. The magical sixteenth, the sweetest day of all a young lady could look forward to. Supposedly, the awkwardness of the early teens and the self-doubts disappeared in the night, so when you awakened that morning you were to behold the bloom of womanhood.

I lay in my four-poster bed admiring the polished, chintz skirt my mother had made for my kidney-shaped dressing table. She had also surprised me with a matching bedspread and bench cover all patterned with tiny white roses on a cherry red background. A new dress, courtesy of many pleadings to my father, was draped over a straight-backed chair. It was a complete change from my usual skirt and blouse ensembles. I had insisted on shopping in the misses department even though I had difficulty finding a dress to fit my junior petite figure.

I finally chose a soft, rust colored crepe de Chine, long sleeved, scooped neckline with a flared skirt cinched with a contoured suede belt. I would borrow my mother's gold chain and I would look sophisticated for my date with Wes tonight.

It was six weeks since my return from camp. Wes had called every day. We also had seen each other several times for cokes and a short drive after school, but this was the first date.

Rather than have a party, as was suggested by my mother, Wes said he would like to take me to the theater. My sister, Vi, heard of his intentions and decided to prepare a grown-up dinner for the two of us and expected us to arrive around seven. Wes picked me up at my house nattily dressed in a tweed jacket, gray slacks with a blue shirt and tie. He handed me a corsage of gardenias, which my mother pinned to my new dress. My hair, freshly washed and shiny, hung loosely to my shoulders still parted in the middle.

"You look absolutely radiant," Wes said as he took my arm. His convertible was parked in front and the neighborhood kids fingered the navy enamel. We had enough time for the half hour drive to Brooklyn Heights.

Vi, a feature writer and her husband Vic, a Federal Courts reporter for the *Brooklyn Eagle,* lived in an apartment on top of a four-story walk-up. Even our young lungs expanded mightily as we reached the last landing.

Vi was waiting at the open door smiling at our efforts. We entered the living room of the one bedroom apartment. The floors were the original parquet from 1842 when this brownstone was originally built. There were Peruvian throw rugs and the walls were hung with prints by Miro and Picasso. The rest of the wall space was taken up with rows of bookcases filled with volumes and interspersed with artifacts.

"Vic had to work tonight," Vi said as she took my coat and led me to the round table she had moved to the windows.

The garret apartment had a breathtaking view of New York Harbor and we could see the lights still coming on. The Brooklyn Bridge looked awesome with its towers lighted against the sky. There were candles glowing on the covered table and a small vase of chrysanthemums. Vi had put out her only two champagne glasses for our ginger ale. I was overwhelmed by her thoughtfulness as Wes pulled out the chair for me.

"Dinner is ready. I know you have plans for the theater, so I'll just be a moment 'til I get the soup," Vi said as she entered the small kitchen.

The brown, steaming thick liquid with the slice of lemon and hard-boiled egg looked totally unfamiliar. "I'm trying out everything new on you two. I hope you don't mind being guinea pigs for my experimentation."

It was black bean soup and we admitted it was delicious. Next came an aromatic platter of chicken curry with raisins, coconut, peanuts and chutney — all interesting flavors making us feel adventurous. "You remembered I love strawberry shortcake," I exclaimed as Vi brought out the dessert.

"What a terrific thing to do for me — you're the best." I hugged her tightly as she was sending us on our way.

"Have a great sixteenth," she called as Wes and I ran down the stairs. Leave it to Vi to do the unusual to make me feel so adult and special.

It was 8:30 by the time we got in the car. "What show are we going to?" I asked as I refreshed my lipstick.

"I hope you don't mind," Wes said as he reached over to put his arm around my shoulder. "I'd like to stop by the St. George Hotel to pick up my camera." That seemed odd to me, but I was feeling so happy I didn't question him.

"My sister is having a party at our house for some cousins and I didn't want to be there when I could be with you," Wes said sensing my bewilderment. "So I decided to take a room at the hotel so I

128

wouldn't have to explain my whereabouts if I got home before they left."

"I'll wait in the car while you get your camera," I said. Wes had been taking a photography class in night shots and he said he wanted to take some of the city lights. "No, I don't want you out here alone. Come up with me and see my room," he said invitingly.

Walking through the lobby I thought every eye was on me — each pair certain I was going to the young man's room for no good purpose. When we got to the elevator I meekly protested, "Perhaps, I should wait here in the lobby."

Wes looked at me adoringly and gently took my hand. "Do what you want, Hon, but you know it's perfectly all right."

The light flashed on floor number 10 and Wes led me out of the elevator down the carpeted, silent, hall to room 1010. He unlocked the door and we entered a small room with a double bed and the spread turned down. There was a bouquet of pink roses on the broad windowsill. The view was the same as Vi's, only higher and more expansive. I noticed a split of champagne on the nightstand with two water glasses. I took in the whole picture and the realization hit me full force that I had been set up for seduction.

Tears stung my eyes, and I blurted out from my sense of betrayal, "How could you do this to me and especially on my 16th birthday?"

Wes took my face in his hands and started kissing my eyes and the tears streaming down my cheeks. "I'm so sorry, Jean, to have upset you. You know I don't think of you as a little girl, but as a beautiful woman," he apologized. "It was thoughtless not to consider you might not be ready for this."

It was now too late to go anywhere. Wes took me in his arms and as he held me I knew he must love me, although he had not yet expressed it in words.

"Before I left my house tonight, I told my sister I had a date with the girl I was going to marry. I think she was startled as I've never said that before about anyone."

He slowly ran his hand down my back to unzip my dress. "Just want to get a little closer and not wrinkle your pretty new outfit. We can lie on the bed or sit on the window seat and look out at the city."

That was a grown-up moment. Should I remain outraged and insist he take me home and risk not seeing him again? Or should I feel flattered that he felt I was woman enough to handle his manly approach?

He sat on the bed awaiting my decision. I looked at his billboard features. His penetrating hazel eyes squinted through the smoke curling up from his filtered cigarette and he gifted me with a tentative perfect smile.

I had no choice.

So, that's how I spent my sixteenth birthday, sitting on the window seat in room 1010 of the St. George Hotel half clothed in a creamy silk slip, in the embrace of my twenty year old boyfriend, who a few hours ago had told his sister I was the girl he was going to marry.

Chapter 20
COURTSHIP

My junior year at Bay Ridge High was full of promise. I was excelling academically and participating in extra curricular activities, especially drama. My favorite English teacher, Mrs. Wagner, would take our special class of 30 young girls to Wednesday matinees on Broadway once a month. We got to meet the actors after the performances and I treasured my autograph book signed by Laurence Olivier, Katherine Hepburn, Ethel Barrymore and other great stars. And how much better could life be when hundreds of envious girls watched as your boyfriend picked you up after school in his navy blue convertible.

Without any official fanfare or gesture towards my parents, the courtship had begun. Now that Wes had set his sights on me, the next step was clearing the decks. I had a few boyfriends I had been seeing occasionally, having met them at dances sponsored by our brother school, Peter Townsend. This came to a halt as Wes suggested I wouldn't need any other male companionship.

It irked my hard-working father that any young man, especially one interested in his daughter, wasn't continuing his education or at least working an honest job. My mother was more sympathetic when I told her that Wes' mother died when he was thirteen and his widowed older sister was bringing him up. His father was a traveling salesman who made up for his prolonged absences with an ample allowance. Rheumatic fever kept Wes bed-ridden for months and he missed his senior year of high school.

During the months of confinement in which Wes read philosophies such as Nietzsche and Schopenhauer, he began to think of himself as a Renaissance man. With no obligations, he could devote himself to the arts, all of which he now wanted to share with me. We went to Carnegie Hall for the debut of Leonard Bernstein's *Capriccio Espanola* and attempted to sit through Wagner's *Valkyrie* at the Metropolitan Opera House. Weekends found us crossing the George Washington Bridge to experience Frank Sinatra at Meadow Brook Inn in New Jersey. Sometimes we double dated with his best friend Sonny and his twenty-year-old girlfriend, Rosalie. Once she cornered me in the ladies' room at a ballroom dance and tauntingly insisted on asking how far our relationship had gone. I could tolerate their smoking and drinking, but personal questions were beyond the limit. Wes obligingly stopped seeing them, which gave us even more time to be alone.

Horseback riding was something we both loved. Some Saturday mornings we'd go to the stables at Prospect Park and go for a morning ride. He'd always choose a frisky, lead horse and I, a docile mare. One beautiful spring morning, we were cantering along the bridle path, when Wes spied two boys ahead of us on bikes.

"What are those kids doing there? I'll give them a lesson they'll never forget," he said, spurring his horse to a full gallop. My mare took off almost immediately in pursuit. Wes was out of sight by the time I reached the panicked boys. Their bikes were out of control as I galloped between them and the wheels ran into my horse's shins. Up she went, neighing and pawing the air in fright. I lost my stirrups and the reins. Coming back to earth, she resumed a gallop and I grabbed onto her mane for dear life. Gradually, I got my arms around her neck and laid my cheek against her sweaty body.

"Slow down, Baby," I kept murmuring, trying to catch my breath. "It's going to be all right."

As soon as the mare regained her stride, I recaptured the reins and slipped my boots back into the stirrups. By this time, we had reached the end of the path and Wes was waiting impatiently. "Where have you been? I thought you were right behind me." He seemed somewhat annoyed.

My eyes were stinging with tears of fury. I was so grateful to still be astride my horse that I didn't feel like saying anything. Yet I wondered what I was getting myself into.

Summer was approaching and we had already made plans for camp. I was going to apply for a junior drama counselor and he would continue as senior swim counselor. It seemed idyllic. However, my parents had other ideas. They had tried to caution me all year about the danger of Wes' exclusivity. But I argued I was keeping up with my studies and I was handling the situation in a mature manner. It came as a blow when I was told I was going to any camp but Shawangee and that was firm.

"I'd rather stay home," I stormed. But that wasn't viable either. Sixteen-year-old girls didn't get jobs in the city, and summer school was for slow learners. A friend, Marion, whom I knew from camp a few years ago, suggested I join her at the one she attended the previous summer. It was in Connecticut, hours away from Pennsylvania where Wes would be. I could get a job there, too, as a junior counselor.

My parents were so eager to separate Wes and me that they never checked out the facility. Camp Neepawa was located near the town of Torrington in a tree-lined acreage with a stagnant lake. It took me a week to fully discover it was run as an orthodox

Hebrew camp. The boys wore yarmulkes, the food was noodle-based and they served fruit soup once a week on Saturdays when the kitchen was closed, to keep all the campers regular. Friday nights there were services, and no activities were planned for Saturdays.

I had a minimal job, which amounted to nothing more than babysitting five unruly eight year olds. I confronted Marion as to why she didn't tell me what I was getting into. But she said it was perfectly fine for her.

"Do you know what kind of camp this is?" I screamed at my parents over the phone. They said all they knew was that it was approved by the Board of Health and that was good enough for them.

I couldn't have been more miserable. My only bright spot was mail call when a daily letter would be awaiting me from Wes. On his day off, the first month, he drove five hours to be with me for one precious hour. I had to get out of there. I dreamed up the perfect solution by which I could make an escape to the city. I systematically ate a whole box of caramels, which eventually loosened all the caps on my braces. The prospect of seeing the dentist was never more pleasurable. When I got home, I pleaded my case again, using all the dramatic tricks I knew, insisting that I simply had to transfer to Shawangee for the second month. There was no way out. All the tuition was paid through the summer.

When I returned to Camp Neepawa, I kept to myself except for a couple of illegal hitchhiking sorties I talked Marion into, so we could go horseback riding in Litchfield. I read, wrote and dreamed of the last day of August. In a desperate attempt for sociability, I became friendly with the young men who worked in the kitchen. They were locals who took me to town on Friday or Saturday nights for a movie or a visit to the neighborhood tavern to dance to the jukebox.

This way I didn't have to attend the weekly folk dancing sessions. They were nice and polite fellows, especially Tom, but all I could think of when I was with one of them was Wes. Besides, even their Old Spice cologne couldn't hide the sour kitchen smell that permeated their skin.

The last day of my internment had been planned as a reunion with Wes. We were to meet that night as we were both returning the same day. My parents said they'd be driving up to get me. I had sent my footlocker ahead and I was waiting expectantly for them at the gate. I jumped into the car hoping for a speedy turnaround, but to my surprise, there was my brother alongside me in the backseat.

Before we even got on our way, my mother said, "We're going to Ithaca to help Laurie find housing for the fall semester. Vi's meeting us there and she's made arrangements for all of us to stay at her old sorority house."

Not knowing how else to deal with this treachery, I gave my brother a swift kick in the shins and turned my head towards the window. En route, we stopped at Delaware Water Gap, a scenic overlook. As I looked hundreds of feet over the rock wall contemplating jumping, a train snaked its way along the river. I convinced myself that it was the train Wes was on heading for Grand Central Station, expecting to soon hold me in his arms. My head started to throb and I had my first ever nosebleed.

That night on the sleeping porch of my sister's sorority house at Cornell, I felt emotional and physical changes taking place inside me. I was full of frustrations and longings to be elsewhere. Somehow, I had to break loose from my parental captivity and Wes had to be the liberator.

Chapter 21
CROSSROADS OF THE WORLD

That September of my senior year, I received a postcard from Doris Dudley, a protégé of Kathryn Graham, inviting me to join her dance classes, I thought it was a message from heaven. A year ago, at camp, I was a devoted student and found this method of expression came naturally to me. After the void of last summer, I longed for an artistic outlet.

"Mother, I'd really like to do this," I said as I showed her the invitation. "Would you help out in paying for the lessons?" She agreed but wondered how my father would react to my missing dinner twice a week to go into Manhattan. I didn't realize how opposed my father actually was until the second week of class. I was on my way to the subway on Thursday evening around 5 when I saw him following me in the car. He pulled over to the curb. "Get in," he said. "Where do you think you are going? You never thought to ask me about taking those lessons." I was surprised at how angry he was. "You don't have to go running off to Manhattan two nights a week. Can't you find something during the day closer to home?"

"Dad, it's an honor to be asked by Doris Dudley to be her student and that's what I'm going to do. I knew you'd give me an argument if I asked you so I'm going to do it, no matter what you say. You don't have to be so angry. Just let me out at the corner. I'm going to be late!"

"I don't know why you don't listen to me anymore," he uttered in desperation. "Just you wait, something's going to happen to you!"

I grabbed my dance bag, slammed the car door and ran towards the subway. I flew down the steps and put my nickel in the turnstile. I slid my way into a car just as the doors were closing. I tried to catch my breath, but I didn't seem able to breathe. My father's last words rang like a curse in my ears. My heart was pounding. I could feel a cold sweat breaking out on my forehead.

"What's happening to me?" I wondered. The people around me seemed to fade in and out. There weren't any empty seats so I held on to a pole to keep from falling. I managed to change to the express train that would take me to 56th Street and Broadway.

"This will pass," I kept telling myself. By the time I found my way to the studio I could hardly make it up the stairs. I changed into my leotards and slippers and went to my place at the barre. Looking in the mirror, I frightened myself seeing this pale, drawn face reflected. It was difficult to say anything, as I didn't know how to express what I felt. I wasn't sick. I just wasn't well. Midway through the class, I couldn't continue, so I went to the changing room to lie down.

"I want to go home," I thought. "But somehow, I don't want to go alone. I'll just wait 'til class is over and walk to the subway with Kit and Marsha. Then I'll be OK."

After I paid for class, I had a nickel left over for the ride home. "It's such a nice evening," Kit said. "Let's walk to 42nd Street."

That's not what my rubbery legs wanted to hear, but I couldn't leave my friends. When we got to 42nd Street, Kit and Marsha hoped I'd be feeling better next time and left for the IRT. I headed for the BMT.

As I started down the steps, the metallic smell of the subway permeated my nostrils. I could even taste it. I tried going further but there appeared a wall — a wall of undefined fear. I couldn't go over it, through it or around it. I returned to the street. I'll try again. The wall appeared at the first step.

"Now what am I going to do?" I was so confused.

On the corner of 42nd Street and Broadway, the crossroads of the world, was a Schulte Cigar store. I went in and with my last and only nickel, I called home.

My father answered the phone. "I'm with a customer. What do you want?"

"Dad, can you come get me? I think I'm sick and I can't get home. I'm in the Schulte Cigar store on 42nd Street and Broadway. I'll wait for you."

"What do you mean, you can't get home. Take the subway. I can't talk right now. Give me your number and I'll call back."

Twenty minutes went by as I sat dejected in the phone booth. Why didn't he call? I had no money to try again.

I could see the proprietor at the counter talking to a customer. He was wearing a gray and white striped shirt with garters holding up the sleeves. He had a round face like the logos on the cigar bands. I stared at his face as I approached the counter and softly pleaded, "Could you please lend me 5 cents to call my father? I used up all my money and I need to have him come for me. I'll pay you back then."

What he must have seen was a pretty, teenage girl in a sweater and skirt and bobbie socks somehow making no sense at all. He looked at me as though I was invisible. He didn't bother to answer, but turned back to his conversation with the man.

I crawled back to the glass-enclosed phone booth prepared to die. Then, through my tears, I glimpsed a cab waiting at the curb. I had never taken a cab but it beckoned as my salvation.

I poured out my tale to the driver and begged him if he would only take me to Brooklyn Heights where my sister lived, he would be paid in full. "Sure, get in," he said. "I gotta daughter your age and I hope somebody would help her, too. Besides, I'm off duty so I can go across the bridge on my own time."

I stood in the dark hallway of the aged brownstone and with trembling fingers, rang the bell. Thank goodness, Vi and Vic were home. Vic thanked the cabbie profusely as he paid the fare.

As I repeated my story, as best I could, we tried to find a logical reason for what had happened. Vi had taken a psychology minor at college and assured me that I had probably experienced a nervous upset. After sharing a hot cup of tea and a couple of biscuits, it was time to go. And in keeping with the old adage of getting on the horse that threw you, Vic gave me an *Esquire* magazine and walked me to the nearest subway. "Call me when you get home. You'll be fine."

I climbed the stairs in darkness. I went to my room, locked the door and cried myself to sleep. I knew Vi had most likely called my mother, but I didn't want to talk to anyone — especially my father — ever.

That should have been the end of it but the evil genie was out of the bottle. The next Tuesday evening I tried to go to class, but couldn't get past the first stop before I had to return. I found it becoming uncomfortable to walk to school or sit in class.

One night I was home alone. I had done my homework and gone to bed. I lay there thinking of why I should have trouble on the subway when there were people all around and yet was able to be calm alone in the house with no one to call on. What a suggestion that was! Alone! How alone could I be? What if I became deathly ill and no one was here? Then it came as if called — the pounding heart, the cold sweat, the shortness of breath, the adrenalin rush. I got out of bed and put on all the lights. I turned the radio up loud and paced all the rooms. Luckily, my parents came home shortly afterwards.

My world was closing in on me. I couldn't stay alone in the house. Food wouldn't stay down. Sleep left me and in its place, night tremors. During this intense time, when Wes called, I'd say, "Hold on I'll be right back," and I'd go to vomit. I was losing weight rapidly yet no one knew what to do about me. My mother was deeply concerned and prayed with me at night. The doctor prescribed belladonna for my upset stomach and said it was an adolescent phase I was going through.

In October, Wes informed me that he was applying to the Air Corps for pilot training. He didn't want to be drafted so he had to figure out a way to not only get a GED, as he never finished high school, but to also pass an equivalency test of two years of college. Remarkably, with the help of a tutor, in 6 weeks he learned calculus and trigonometry, meeting all the requirements. He was accepted into the Air Corps flight program and even passed the physical despite his rheumatic heart.

The prospect of Wes' leaving added to my anxieties. He had become a daily presence in my life practically to the exclusion of anyone else. I had come to believe that I needed him to live and breathe.

On Sunday, December 7, 1941, my mother and father and I were in the living room listening to the Texaco Theater presentation from the Metropolitan Opera. In the middle of the performance, the announcement came through that the Japanese had bombed Pearl Harbor. The war had started. It was an incendiary to the war that had already started within me. In 2 weeks, Wes left for Alabama. Much to my surprise, I began to mend.

Chapter 22
I DO, I DO!

The props of the DC3 pierced the clouds sending wisps of white over the wings. My head pressed against the cold Plexiglas as I stared out in wonderment into the starless sky. I was too exhausted by now to feel frightened about being on my first flight and an eight hour one at that. Earlier, I had comforted my mother that I now had Wes to take care of me and we could face anything together. Wes had encouraged me to try to get some sleep while he went forward to talk to the pilots who had invited him into the cockpit.

My thoughts couldn't contain themselves, so I tried to review the past 30 hours as if I were writing in my journal. What was I doing here and how did it all start?

Why doesn't someone answer that phone that's ringing in my sleep? I opened my eyes and saw the radium dial of the Big Ben clock on my dresser. Four-thirty a.m. Who could it possibly be? I found my way in the dark to the dining room, picked up the receiver and sat on the cold radiator. "Hello." All I could hear was muffled background noise.

"Hi, Hon, I'm at the Atlanta airport ready to board a flight to New York."

"You're what?"

"Just listen to what I have to say. Got a pencil? I don't have much time. I'll be arriving at Idyllwild at 11:00 this morning. I left the base this afternoon in the trunk of a buddy's car, got a train to Jacksonville then to Atlanta. We have to get married today so I can be back on base for check-in Monday morning."

"But that's impossible. I can't arrange everything so quickly."

"Look, I know you can do it. This may be the only chance before I'm sent overseas. Gotta go, Hon. Love you with all my heart. By the way, you did get your blood test as we planned? I have my Alabama one. See you in a few hours, Mrs. Warner." Click.

I sat on the cold radiator shivering in my cotton nightie. How could this be happening? Of course, I wanted to marry Wes, but not like this. I wanted a traditional wedding — a white gown with a train and flowers everywhere — all eyes on me walking down the aisle to my Air Corps groom.

My parents interrupted my daydream. "What's going on? Who called?"

When I explained they both agreed (one of the rare times in my lifetime) that the whole idea was beyond the realm of reason. He'd just have to wait for a more appropriate time. Here we were. My parents and I in our nightclothes, still in the predawn darkness, about to embark on the argument of the century: whether it was advisable for me to get married within the next fourteen hours.

Bold determination immediately set in. I wasn't asking permission to go to the movies or buy a new coat. I had been given orders from a fighter pilot who had just been knighted with silver wings to serve his country — "to live in fame or go down in flames."

"What about school? You just started college. You're not even eighteen. Jeanie, what's the rush? What if he gets killed?"

I had abandoned the dreams of going to Cornell as my sister and brother did before me. Wes had begged me to stay close and go to Brooklyn College so he could see me when on leave.

"Remember when Vi wrote to you, Dad, about the movie, *Mrs. Miniver?* In wartime it isn't necessarily the soldier who gets killed. You know we're in love. I've known Wes for two years and he needs to be assured I'll be waiting for him while he's risking his life for his country."

What a noble statement! Deep down I was terrified, wanting the phone call to have been an illusion. I didn't want to deal with this. Why couldn't we be engaged and take our chances that all would be well? And college. I really wanted to be at Cornell away from the city and the frightening air raid drills that sent us huddled in the hallways until the sirens' all clear. But I owed Wes my loyalty. He had impressed this point on me the last time he was home on leave in August, when we went to Vermont with his father and stepmother. I had confronted him with all the objections to such an early marriage, but he was a born master of persuasion. Again, I had no choice but to go forward as if it were what I wanted most in my life. To say "no" would be tantamount to losing him.

"Mother, Dad, somehow Wes and I are going to be married today. So, I ask you to please give me your blessings. I don't know how it's going to happen and I'll need your cooperation. You both know how scared I am right now, so just for once help me see this through as a family."

I'll never forget that moment. We three embraced as never before. My mother, the romanticist, shed tears of love; my father, the pragmatist, held back tears of frustration and I, the child, shed tears of gratitude for their understanding mixed with fear of the unknown.

Whenever a question of import arose, the only one to call was my sister, Vi. By 7:30, I had presented her with the enigma of how to perform the miracle of bringing about a wedding in less than twelve hours. She said she'd discuss it with Vic and get back to us as soon as possible. By 9:00, Vic was on the phone. With his connection to City Hall, he had worked out a feasible plan of action. The Marriage License Bureau closed at noon in downtown New York and wouldn't be open Monday, Columbus Day. He had arranged for them to remain open fifteen minutes longer than usual, acting on the emergency of a serviceman on a weekend pass before going overseas. In order to get there on time, a police escort, courtesy of Mayor LaGuardia, would meet Wes at Idyllwild and the two of us would be accompanied to City Hall where Vic would meet us.

I had less than an hour to pick out from my closet what might be my wedding outfit.

"Mother, if I wear my navy suit can I borrow your white coat?"

Was this a picture of a bride I saw in the mirror? The navy form-fitting jacket had a trim of red blanket stitches. I chose patent leather pumps and carried an envelope purse of black patent and red leather. I wore my mother's white wool coat over my shoulders so it wouldn't look too large for my frame. As I reached for my gloves, I decided to pin a bunch of white artificial hyacinths into my dark hair.

When I left the house that morning with my father on the way to the airport, I knew my life would never be the same. As much as I was caught up in the drama and excitement, something powerful inside wanted to remain Jeanie forever. It seemed my whole family had reluctantly assumed roles in perpetuating an outcome about which none of us were certain.

At Idyllwild, two of New York's Finest approached Wes as he stepped onto the tarmac anxiously looking for me behind the gate.

"We've been assigned, Lieutenant, to escort you and your fiancée to City Hall," one of the policemen stated formally. "Just follow us to your fiancée's car and we'll precede you on our motorcycles into town."

Even with a surprised expression on his face, Wes looked like a model for an Air Corps recruiting poster — the cocked angle of his hat, his khaki jacket sprouting his silver wings and still creased officer's pinks. All my doubts disappeared.

"How's my beautiful bride? Sorry to throw this at you so unexpectedly, but there were rumors about getting orders next week. I couldn't leave without knowing I had you all to myself as my wife, my love."

How unbelievable this part of the scenario seemed. Wes and I were together in the back seat in our dream state, my father driving the car so his young daughter and persistent suitor could get a marriage license, while outside the sirens from the police cycles were parting the traffic like Moses at the Red Sea. Across the boulevards of Queens, over the 59th Street Bridge, down Park Avenue to the southern tip of Manhattan, my father never exceeded 35 miles per hour. Police or not, there was no way he would go over the speed limit.

At 12:20, our motorcade pulled up to the steps of City Hall. Vic was waiting impatiently looking at his watch. As we entered the marble lobby, the maintenance people were mopping the floors.

"Everyone's gone 'til Tuesday. Nothing's open in the building," a janitor said wringing out his mop. "Why don'tcha try Brooklyn. Maybe it's them that got the message."

Back to the car and like a Keystone Cops movie, off we went over the Brooklyn Bridge, this time with Wes at the wheel and Vic beside him. In five minutes, we were at City Hall. Vic said to wait while he inquired inside. The expression on his face when he returned told the whole story.

"I think we better have a realistic discussion about what our options are, if any," he began soberly. "First, you can't get a marriage certificate today; secondly, Wes' Alabama blood test is not valid in New York State and if you can't wait until Tuesday — right now it appears impossible. We'd better let the police escorts go." Vic paused. "However, I still might have one hope."

"Here, take the keys," said my frazzled father. "I've had enough and I'm going home on the subway. It's Saturday, you know, and I've got to get back to the store. If anything changes, call." And with that, he gave me a peck on the cheek and walked away shaking his head. I never felt so much love for that man.

"Now this might sound crazy," Vic went on. "But I know a judge who hangs out at the Hotel Bossert bar regularly. If I can tell him a good enough story we could find a way to cut through all this red tape."

There was no way to back out now. We had to follow the next lead. There was no doubt in Wes' mind that all was going to work out. "Doesn't true love always conquer?"

It seemed hours before Vic returned to the car, his flushed face matching his red hair.

"Okay, this is the deal. It's 2 o'clock now. Judge Taylor said to meet him in his chambers at 4. Call Mother and Dad and have them there also as both must sign since you're not eighteen. There's a loophole for servicemen's marriages in the Domestic Relations Act of New York State and this will allow the blood test to be waived. I've already called Vi and she'll meet us here in a few minutes. She wants to help you buy a wedding dress since Mother and she cooked up a ceremony for you at home tonight. I've got work to do now since I'll have to retype the whole section before it can be signed, so don't thank me yet. Judge Taylor has been known not to keep appointments, depending on how long he's been at the bar."

Wes held me tightly. "As soon as Vi gets here, I'm going to get you a ring and I'll meet you at the Judge's office at a quarter to four."

What I didn't know was that Vi and Mother had decided that morning that it wouldn't be fitting to get married at City Hall with no one in attendance. So, between them they were able to locate a rabbi to placate my father, contact as many relatives as were available and set up a reception and dinner at the St. George Hotel at 8:30 p.m.

Vi told me all this as we chose a pearl gray, two piece, velvet wedding suit. The saleswoman found a stovepipe hat to match and draped a soft gray veil over it. As we had no time for lunch and I was feeling faint, we stopped for tea in the department store.

"Are you all right, little sister? I hope you want this with your whole being, because we're moving mountains to get this done. You know how Dad feels, yet he's truly being remarkable."

At 3:45, we all assembled at Judge Taylor's mahogany paneled chambers. Vic had been given the key and he'd been busily at work at the typewriter. At 4:00 p.m. sharp, the Judge appeared wearing a brown cardigan sweater. He greeted us all by name and seated himself in the leather chair behind his massive desk.

"I'm always pleased to help out my constituents, especially under such circumstances as these. Congratulations, Lieutenant Warner, on achieving your pilot's wings, and if it's yours and Jeanie's desire to marry — so be it. My job is to see that the law doesn't stand in the way of true love. By the way, if you would like a drink while we're waiting for Vic to finish I'd be glad to join you."

We declined, and shortly Vic had the papers ready for signing by the bride and groom, Vi and Vic as witnesses, my parents' release, and the judge waiving the necessity of a blood test and a three day waiting period.

"All I have to do now," he said jovially, "is to say, 'by the power invested in me by the State of New York, I now pronounce you man and wife.' May I kiss the bride?" The smell of whiskey can be overpowering when the receiver is in a fragile state. This man, however, had pulled out all the stops, so I gratefully accepted his full mouth kiss.

It would have been a relief to go off by ourselves now that we were legally married, but, for some, the day had barely begun. Wes went home to rest and freshen up. I left with my folks to collapse physically and mentally before my next wedding at 7:30 p.m.

My dear mother had baked all afternoon and made hors d'oeuvres for the unknown number of relatives who might arrive. I had never been instructed on the procedure of a Jewish wedding and Wes hadn't the slightest idea either. I realized this was a gesture of good will on our part and, as I was a quick study, we could both wing it.

About 25 people showed up, some from Wes' side of the family I had never met. Vi was my Maid of Honor and since Wes couldn't locate his closest friend, he asked Vic to be his Best Man. My brother Laurie's fiancée, Judy, was a bridesmaid. As the bride and groom stood under the archway in the living room, my mother played the Wedding March from Tannhauser. Just then the front door bell rang.

"It's your friend, Judy Lang," my brother reported. "She wants to know if you can go to the movies?"

"I'll be right back, everybody," and ran down the stairs. "Oh, Judy, what perfect timing! Would you believe I'm getting married this minute and I must have you for a bridesmaid. You're my dearest friend."

"Look at me. I'm in my saddle shoes. I don't feel right."

"Please, it'll mean so much to me. Come on, the Rabbi is waiting."

For the second time that day I heard, "By the power that's vested in me by the State of New York, I now pronounce you man and wife." Instead of being offered whiskey, I was given a glass of wine to share with my new husband who then (according to instructions) smashed it to pieces under a towel.

I remember little of the dinner reception at the hotel. I couldn't eat, I was exhausted. I must have responded to the many toasts with wine so when we excused ourselves at 11 o'clock, I was more ready for a good night's sleep than the bridal chamber. After all, I had been up since 4:30 a.m., married twice, drank too much and that seemed enough for one day.

We weren't in room 1010 of the same hotel as we were on my sixteenth birthday, when Wes had first tried to seduce me, but the bridal suite after two years of courtship. And amazingly, I was still as intact as I was then. After I had rejected his advances several times, Wes convinced himself that it would be the height of romanticism for him to marry a virgin.

What I do recall of our wedding night was that we read the Sunday funnies aloud to each other, I threw up, and we fell asleep like two worn out children until we both awakened at 3 a.m. to consummate our wedding vows and again at 5.

When I came out of the bathroom in the morning, Wes was on the phone. I could hear him say a girl's name over and over. "But Francine, but Francine, you knew it wasn't like that between us. I just thought I should let you know. Gotta go now, bye."

"Who was that, Wes? Who's Francine and why are you calling her this morning?"

"Okay, now don't get mad. It's like this. You really owe her. How'd you think I kept you pure all this time? You think I didn't need an outlet for all the passion you brought out? Francine was always there for me. Besides, her mother made the best lemon meringue pie on Long Island. But I never loved her."

Wes could see the shock and horror on my face. I felt like throwing up again. "Why do you always toss me a curve? You think you can do anything just so long as you say you love me! Why didn't you marry Francine?"

"Because she's not beautiful and smart like you and I don't want to spend the rest of my life with her. You don't understand that sex doesn't always have to have anything to do with love. A man knows that. Forgive me. Now that I have you, I'll never need anyone else ever again, I swear it. Come on now, Hon, we have lots of things to do before we leave tonight for Tallahassee. But right now I can only think of one, Mrs. Lieutenant Warner."

Wes slipped back into his aisle seat. "Did I awaken you?" he said "The pilot just told me we made such good time, we'll be landing twenty minutes early. We should be at the hotel by 10:30. Tomorrow we'll look for housing in town. Even if it's only for a few weeks, we'll make every minute count."

It was 6 a.m. when Wes left for his BOQ at the airbase to make it seem as if he had never been gone. By 10 o'clock, I had eaten breakfast and was sitting reading a magazine on the veranda of the old plantation hotel not knowing when Wes would return. I felt like a displaced person in a foreign land, never having been far from New York. Tallahassee looked more like pictures I had seen of the Carolinas than Florida, with not a palm tree in sight. By noon, I was becoming panicky not having heard from Wes. I was about to inquire at the desk when I saw him coming up the walkway. He had a sheepish look on his face.

"Guess what, Hon, when I reported in this morning the Sergeant said, "Warner, you lucky SOB, you've got a ten day leave waiting for you. Now you can go home and get married!"

Chapter 23
THE HONEYMOON

The next morning found us on a Greyhound bus headed back to New York. It seemed like the logical way to spend the ten days that unexpectedly appeared. After two days of travel, we arrived just in time to attend the wedding reception of Wes' stepsister, Dorothy.

'Do we really have to make an appearance?"I pleaded. "You look spiffy in your uniform—but look at me—I look like a little brown church mouse."

Despite my objections, Wes hailed a cab that took us to the Waldorf-Astoria Hotel.

As we entered the grand ballroom, the lovely bride was greeting the guests in a designer white, satin gown, covered with seed pearls, while manipulating a train that looked 1/4 mile long. A banquet table lined one mirrored wall, laden with opened gifts that repeated themselves in the reflection. White linen-coated waiters served the crowd champagne and fancy hors d'ouvres.

I couldn't help thinking if Wes hadn't been so impatient, I too, could have had a real wedding but would have wanted nothing on this scale.

One day during our stay, Wes said he would be gone for a few hours and would return with a surprise for me. It surely was. "I have to blindfold you now. No peeking," he said as he led me to the street at my parent's house. When he uncovered my eyes it was hard to believe what I saw. No more bus or plane for us. He had taken our wedding money and bought us a used Ford convertible to drive back to Florida. That three-day road trip was to be our honeymoon.

When we returned to Tallahassee, we had only a few days left to find a place to live. Rentals were at a premium as there was no base housing. In a quiet residential neighborhood, we were lucky to find what we needed. The lady who owned the house provided us with a bedroom, private bath, door to a nice backyard and one shelf of her refrigerator.

Life settled into somewhat of a routine with waiting daily for overseas orders as a big part of it.

Wes left early each morning for training at the base but would come home for lunch when he could. I'd fix sandwiches to eat in the backyard. They were long days for me as I didn't drive and it was quite a walk to town. There was only one other married couple in the squadron and we became close friends. Meg and Jay shared many events with us, like my 18th birthday at the Officer's Club. Jay was there to separate Wes from attacking a fellow pilot who he thought was holding me too close as we danced. Meg was there to help when Wes was restricted to the base for 2 weeks for buzzing me in his P 47 fighter plane while I was hanging out clothes. I could see him in the cockpit, waving and smiling as he waggled his wings. Someone got the numbers off his plane and reported him.

After three months, the orders arrived. All dependents were to leave within 48 hours. We had been living on the edge for so long but when it finally happened, it was still a shock. This time it was for real. We had to say our goodbyes, maybe forever.

Wes took me to the airport, assuring me all the way, "This parting isn't the end for us. I'll write every day. Our love will get us through it all." Tearfully, I climbed aboard the commuter plane that was to take me to Atlanta. There I boarded a DC8 for New York. I was seated next to a gentleman who saw my distress and for the next four hours, provided me with tales and good humor making the trip bearable. He even insisted on staying with me until he handed me over to my waiting father.

"Oh, Daddy, here I am again," I said sobbing into his shoulder like a child.

"Come on, let's go to the lounge where you can relax." He ordered two brandies.

"You know I don't drink."

"Just take sips. That's my cure-all for tensions."

The brandy did its work. It was hard to imagine myself sitting in a bar having a drink with my father and sharing in adult conversation.

"It's time to go home. Mother has made your favorite dinner," he said putting out his cigar.

As we drove, a light snow had started to fall. He dropped me off in front of the house before going to the garage.

I opened the door and stepped into the vestibule. That wonderful smell said it all.

Pot roast.

Chapter 24
RETURN TO TALLAHASSEE

Home. How strange it all felt. Three months ago I had left as a child-bride and here I was again in familiar surroundings that seemed totally alien. My name had changed to Mrs. Warner, but deep down why did I sense I was still a fearful child?

Wes had been calling at least twice a day forlornly protesting how much he missed me. "Nothing is happening here. No rumors, no further preparations. I can't stand this waiting game."

Then, the pleading started. "Can't you come back? It could be weeks before we pull out. I need you so much."

"But, Wes, it was so difficult to leave and I've only been home less than a week. There's no way I can even get transportation. I miss you, too, but I just can't do it."

Another day, "I can't bear the thought of maybe never seeing you again. I beg you. See what can be done. I know there are ways."

The prospect of Wes spending his last days before combat pining away out of loneliness for me was breaking down my defenses. Again, I knew he was asking an almost impossible feat from me. Just getting back from Tallahassee had been a monumental step, scared all the way, and now I was being pressured (by love, of course) to return — even if only for a few days.

"Mother, Dad, what should I do?"

"It's rare for you to come to us for an opinion these days," my father said as we were at the dinner table.

"It's a difficult decision to make, but you have to do it yourself," Mother contributed. "However, as it happens just today Daddy decided to join Paul Neilsen on a business trip to Florida and they are leaving Thursday. Maybe, they could take you as far as Jacksonville."

"You didn't tell me about this, Daddy. Do you think we could do it? Do you think I could get a ticket?"

It was suddenly becoming plausible.

The reservation agent on the phone confirmed that there were no seats available for that day or any day in the near future. Not even priority. But by now, Paul Neilsen, my father's traveling friend and competitor in the furniture business and a cagey wheeler-dealer, was intrigued by the idea. He was a tall, stocky, ruddy-faced Dane, full of adventure and a hearty drinker for whom nothing was impossible.

"Tell Jeanie to be ready to go and we'll take care of the rest."

When Wes called again that evening, I told him the news that I would be arriving 12 noon in Jacksonville on Friday. I didn't know the details such as the train number, but I would expect him to be there when I arrived. He was ecstatic.

"I knew you'd come through! I even rented a room in a beautiful house in the hills. Wait 'til you see it. This is so great. See you Friday, my love."

When the realization set in, I turned cold and started to tremble. How can I do this? At least I'd have company on the way down and I just can't worry about anything beyond that. As soon as Dad and Paul turn me over to Wes, it'll all work out, I assured myself.

My mother fully understood my concerns. It was she who was always there to comfort and allay my fears. It was she who cradled my head in her lap when I was a child and slept with me in later years when the night attacks kept my body convulsing. She would sing hymns and say prayers with me until the demons left. She knew my agonies, yet when I made a forthright decision, she never questioned it. Nevertheless, she was continually amazed at my bravery.

Early Friday morning, the yellow cab drove up with Paul beaming in the back seat. Mother hugged me and whispered an assurance of God's protection and gave me a copy of the Christian Science Journal. We were off to Pennsylvania Station.

It was a snowy January day, so I was dressed appropriately for a New York winter. I was wearing a forest green two-piece wool suit, a white silk blouse, and an ocelot fur jacket with hat to match. I had a suitcase, a leather handbag and a cosmetic carrying case.

At the station, Paul reviewed the strategy he had devised in the taxi. Since I didn't have a ticket, what was needed was a diversionary tactic so I could get through the gate. Paul would distract the ticket agent so that Dad and I could make our way to the train without being stopped. He said he would catch up with us. It worked perfectly and we boarded the train to Washington with ease.

Paul arrived and gave me his ticket while he headed off for the club car. All Dad had to do after the agent cleared us was to go to the club car and return the ticket to Paul. Even though it was punched, he succeeded in maneuvering the agent to let it pass.

The Silver Meteor to Miami was just across the platform when we arrived in Washington, D.C. Though it wasn't part of the plan, leaving my jacket on the New York train worked to our advantage. Paul went back to get it while Dad and I did the ticket switch. Since this was going to be a long overnight trip and we would all need accommodations, we decided to confess our predicament to the head porter.

"My daughter," explained my father, "has to get to Jacksonville because her pilot husband is being sent overseas and she may never see him again. I'll give her my seat and sit in the club car with my friend. We'll pay you for the price of the ticket."

The head porter looked us over, especially me, who by this time must have been showing signs of strain, and said, "I'm not supposed to do this, but I'll see you all get taken care of. I can't take no money for the ticket, but it don't say nowhere that a tip wouldn't be acceptable."

Gladly, my Dad did just that.

I didn't see much of my father and Paul after that. They had started their vacation and were more interested in swapping stories and sharing their brandy and cigars. I read and tried to sleep, feeling so deserted in this train packed with people.

"Just think of tomorrow," I kept telling myself. "Wes will be there and he'll take care of you from then on."

The train was only an hour late pulling into the Jacksonville station. Dad and Paul helped me with my suitcase and belongings onto the platform. My heart was racing as I looked everywhere for Wes. The platform was teeming with servicemen and civilians so I figured he would be appearing anytime now. It had only been about ten minutes when they were calling the "All Aboard."

"Sorry to leave you, but we have to go," my father said reluctantly. "I'm sure he'll be here soon. Goodbye, Jeanie." And he gave me a peck on the cheek. Paul waved from the steps and the Silver Meteor started down the tracks.

I stood transfixed, people jostling me from every side. The hot sun, bringing the temperature up to 85 degrees, penetrated my wool suit and my ocelot jacket hung on my arm as if it were still attached to the animal. I must have stayed in that position for a half hour, not allowing myself to move in case Wes came looking for me. Something was very wrong or he would be here.

It took all the energy I could muster to find an empty pay phone to see if I could call the air base. The operator intercepted and said all the phone lines were down between Jacksonville and Tallahassee and to try back later in the day. I called for a train schedule and found there were no trains for two days. The airlines were no better and I couldn't find a number for the bus. For all intents and purposes, I could have been stranded in Bombay. I had no idea of what to do next. I was beyond panic, no options, and I didn't even know what questions I should ask anyone.

I sat on my suitcase and was at the depths of despair when I noticed the rolled up Journal in my jacket pocket. It occurred to me that there are Christian Science practitioner listings for every city in the back pages. I peeled the sticky pages open and under Florida was Jacksonville and a listing of several names. I chose one that was in the downtown area and placed a call.

How sweet and encouraging was the voice that answered. "Don't take time to explain your problem. Just take a cab and come to the 5th floor of the Lynch Building. I'll be waiting for you."

Hope! I had made human contact and she gave me hope. I took the elevator to the 5th floor, which turned out to be a Christian Science Reading Room. The practitioner had an office in the same suite.

The kindest, most beautiful, middle-aged lady lovingly approached me, took one look and inquired, "When have you eaten last?" She unloaded my hands and arms, led me to a restroom, and gave me a fluffy towel. "Take care of your needs," she said gently. "I'll have a sandwich and milk for you when you come out and then we will talk."

After we introduced ourselves — her name was Mrs. Barker — I proceeded to relate my odyssey and how I happened to be in her office.

"You look tired, child. Why don't you lie down in the alcove and I will do my work. Just know that God governs us all."

As I lay there on the damask settee, for the first time in days I felt so safe and cared for. "I never want to leave here," I thought.

Within fifteen minutes, Mrs. Barker was calling softly, "Jeanie, I have your husband on the phone."

I picked up the receiver. "Wes, is that you? Where are you? What happened?" I asked in disbelief.

He then proceeded, after expressing much relief that I was all right, to explain that all personnel were restricted to base. He had tried every way he could, short of going AWOL again, but this time the results would have been severe and he couldn't get a pass. He had been frantic not knowing where I was or how we would make contact. If he hadn't walked into the Ward Room just as the call came through, they never would have known where to find him.

"Mrs. Barker said she reserved a seat for you on the 3:30 bus that will arrive into Tallahassee at 11:30 tonight. I swear to you, I will be there. I love you."

I sat down in the wicker chair utterly amazed. "How is this possible? The lines were down. He was unreachable."

Mrs. Barker smiled knowingly and showed me a paragraph in an opened book on her desk, "Science and Health with Key to the Scriptures," by Mary Baker Eddy. It read, "If Spirit (God) pervades all space, it needs no material method for the transmission of messages. Spirit needs no wires nor electricity in order to be omnipresent."

"This is what I worked with. Now, your odyssey is not finished yet. You have to be on that bus in a half hour. A taxi is waiting downstairs."

With tears of gratitude, I embraced Mrs. Barker and vowed I would never forget her.

The taxi dropped me off in the industrial part of town in front of a garage. The only bus waiting there was a yellow school bus. People were already lining up to board. They were dressed in cool, cotton clothes, some carrying bulging string bags and an occasional valise tied with straps. I would have been wearing my checkered sundress too, if Wes had been there to pick me up. What an oddity I must have seemed — all outfitted for a blizzard.

The white people boarded first and when their section was filled, they let the colored occupy the back seats, which had folded down planks across the aisles to make more sitting room.

I checked with the driver to make sure the bus was going to Tallahassee. "No, we're going to Lake City where you'll have to transfer to another bus. That's about two hours from here."

I sat in the front, as I couldn't drag my suitcase, carrying case, ocelot coat with matching hat, any further. Buoyed by the remarkable happenings of the last hour and the encouragement and faith brought on by the meeting with Mrs. Barker, I was prepared for the eight-hour trip ahead. There was no fan on the bus, just an open window bringing in extra heat and dust.

We made it to the crossroads and stopped at a service station that had a food counter. "You best have somethin' to eat here. There ain't nuthin' up ahead for six hours, " a grandfatherly man in patched overalls said as he placed his cracked leather valise next to my suitcase.

I tried to swallow a grilled cheese sandwich, but it stuck in my throat like road tar. Shortly, our gunmetal bus pulled up straight from an army depot and only three of us boarded — the grandfather, a colored man and myself. The stern-faced driver in uniform took my suitcase and loaded it in the side of the bus.

I chose to sit near the door again on the maroon vinyl seat that felt more like a wooden bench. The doors closed and it was like being seated in a coffin. I would just have to trust that I could survive the journey. Shortly, we were driving through the panhandle of Florida, as vast a desert as the West. As far as the eye could see, there was nothing but scrub and palmetto brush. Mercifully, as the sun went down, it began to cool off, but then we were plunged into overwhelming darkness. The driver kept the lights on until 7 o'clock then decided his passengers needed sleep as the grandfather was already snoring mightily.

I couldn't read, I couldn't look at the scenery, there was no one to talk to. I was being catapulted through space without even a star to guide us. The only light was a feeble glow from the dashboard.

The sign over the driver's head read, "DO NOT SPEAK TO OPERATOR WHEN BUS IS IN MOTION." If I could speak to him, I imagined, I would say, "Do you know I have been traveling for over two days and am wearing the same clothes I wore when I left New York? I haven't slept or had a decent meal in that time. I haven't spoken to anyone in hours and I'm so weary. I have no idea where I am. All I know is that out there are only wild rabbits and rattlesnakes. Not a light in a house or a roadside stop. I'm on my way to meet my pilot husband who will probably depart tomorrow for the European Theater of Operations leaving me behind again to find my way home. It would be nice if you could say something to me just to verify that I am here."

I leaned my face against the cool glass window and started to sing softly all the hymns I could remember. A favorite, "Abide with me, fast falls the eventide. The darkness deepens, Lord with me abide. When other helpers fail and comforts flee, Help of the helpless, O, abide with me."

Yes, I could survive this journey. Everything comes to an end.

We pulled into the bus depot in Tallahassee at 11:45 p.m. Wes was there with flowers and a big grin. I stepped off the bus in my forest green two piece wool suit, my silk blouse covered with train soot and road dust, dragging my ocelot fur jacket with matching hat and carrying my cosmetic case. I went to the side of the bus, quickly claimed my suitcase, and then finally collapsed into his waiting arms.

Chapter 25
NEITHER FISH NOR FOWL

It was well after midnight when we drove into the circular driveway of the house where Wes had rented a room. In keeping with the latter part of my journey, I still didn't know where we were except it was several miles out of town.

I was so worn out that I didn't take any notice of my surroundings, so I was pleasantly surprised when I awakened in the morning to see it was indeed as beautiful as Wes had described. Wes was in the shower when I became aware I was in a four-posted bed, the kind with carved pineapples on each post. The rich mahogany wood was highly polished, as were the other pieces of furniture in the room. French doors were open leading to a small balcony from which I could see the tops of stately, old oaks covered with Spanish moss.

"Get up, you sleepy head," Wes urged as he came out of the bathroom and kissed my eyes. "Our landlady, Mrs. Sorenson, has included breakfast every day as part of the rent."

It didn't take me long to bathe and dress as I had developed a huge hunger for home-cooked food. I remembered coming up the stairs the night before, but now as we came out of our room, I found we were on a balcony overlooking a large center hall. Much to my amazement, there were a series of gargoyles along the railing.

At breakfast, we met Mr. Sorenson. He was an architect and had designed and built this extraordinary house out of lumber from rare trees from Jamaica. The gargoyles were an inspiration from the ones on the Notre Dame Cathedral in Paris.

After breakfast, Wes had to report to the base even though it was Sunday, but he promised he wouldn't be gone too long. This gave me a chance to visit further with the Sorensons and see the rest of the grounds. I told them how much we appreciated them offering us a place to stay, especially since we had no idea how long it might be.

In the beginning, it was very tense, but after a week, we began to believe the honeymoon would last forever. But just to be safe, I sent home most of the things in my suitcase so it would be light enough for me to carry when the time came for me to leave. As days went by, Wes and I did have time for ourselves. He had to report in daily for a few hours, but they were no longer doing training missions. We took several short trips to swim at Wakulla Springs, where the Tarzan movies were made. We had dinners with the only other married couple in the squadron, Meg and Jay Marshall from Atlanta. We had become quite close.

"Since I'm still pulling duty and it looks like I won't be going with the squadron, I'll keep my ears open so I can pass on any information that comes my way," Jay offered at dinner one night. "Meg and I will be glad to look after Jean if you have to leave suddenly."

Sure enough, the next day, Jay called. "Something's up for sure, so perhaps you should get ready to leave on a moment's notice. I can't tell you any more than that, but Meg will be over in just a little while."

Wes was there when Meg showed up at the house. She seemed really excited about the news when she explained that Wes and I could be together all the way to New York. Jay had found out the time and method of transportation for the squadron. All the movements were top secret so it was almost an act of espionage to secure the information needed to know what train to meet at the appropriate time. He was sure the orders would be in that night.

We had been dreading this moment for so long, but now that it had come, it was almost a relief. This wasn't going to be our last night together, Wes assured me. Jay would see to that.

The call came through at 10 P.M., informing Lt. Warner to report at 0500. I immediately called my mother to forewarn her that I would somehow be home by train that weekend. I was glad to hear my Dad had just returned from Florida the day before.

"Now don't worry, Hon," Wes comforted me as he lifted his B4 bag on his shoulder. "Meg will be here at 7 a.m. to take you to the station. It'll only be a matter of hours before we'll see each other again, so there's no need for a tearful goodbye."

I was all dressed and packed by 6 a.m. I went out onto the balcony to await the dawn of another day of unwanted adventure. The words and confidence of Mrs. Barker filled my thoughts and I began to feel more hopeful. There was an old Bible on the dresser and I went in to look up the 91st Psalm. I was deep in meditation when I heard Meg drive up.

"Now this is what Jay told me to tell you," Meg reported as we pulled up at the station. "I'll stay with you until the train arrives at 8 a.m. Then you are to board the third car from the engine." Meg was enjoying her role as co-conspirator. I couldn't help but be nervous praying that all would work out as planned. It seemed like an eternity until we heard the sound of the train approaching the station. My heart was pounding in my throat as Meg hugged me and wished me good luck. "Stay in touch," she called out as I made my way to the train.

The regular commuter between Tallahassee and Jacksonville pulled in. Jay said all the pilots would be in civilian clothes so don't be looking for a uniform. As I started to board, I felt my husband's arm assisting me up the steps. We sat by ourselves until Jacksonville where there was to be a transfer to the same Silver Meteor I had taken just 10 days ago.

By the time we arrived in Jacksonville the entire squadron of 18 men knew the plan. As I walked towards the train, they all surrounded me to sneak me aboard and before I knew it, I was in their private car.

It was a scene out of a Gene Tierny movie — an eighteen-year-old heroine, her handsome twenty-two year old pilot husband and seventeen equally young and handsome men off to war in the luxury of a private railroad car. Squadron Commander Bill Riley graciously insisted that Wes and I take his compartment for the duration of the trip.

No one could leave the car so food was sent in. This worked out pretty well until we reached Virginia when the train was forced to remain in its tracks for twelve hours. A huge ice storm had brought down the wires and we were stranded. Luckily, there was a good supply of candy bars that kept us until the next station. And fortunately, I still had my ocelot fur jacket to keep me warm in the unheated car. Besides, how could we mind when this delay gave us extra hours to be together.

I had known most of the pilots from the Officer's Club, but now got to know them even more as brothers. I was pleased that Wes' jealous nature didn't interfere with my playing card games or joining them in singing.

Wes and I spent our last night alone in the compartment. I was grateful for the clickety-clack of the wheels. After all, there were seventeen men outside the door.

At 10 o'clock in the morning we pulled into Pennsylvania Station. First thing I did was to call my parents to ask them to pick me up. Wes and his squadron were told to go to street level to await a bus to take them to an unknown destination. The realization of what was happening began to hit me full force. This wasn't a movie. Wes was really leaving for combat and may never come back. How many of the others would also face that possibility? Spontaneously, the men of the 78th Fighter Squadron lined up and each one, with Wes' permission, kissed me goodbye.

Wes was still there when my parents arrived. It was Sunday, and the store was closed. Wes and I held tightly to each other until his name was called to board the bus. Then the tears started. I wasn't about to restrain them. I stood and waved until the bus rounded the corner of 8th Avenue and 34th Street.

I turned to my parents. They took my bags and put them in the back seat. I sat in the front between my mother and father. My mother took my hand in hers and compassionately extolled me with one of her platitudes.

"Poor Jeanie, neither fish nor fowl."

It didn't take me long to translate this homily, which meant I was no longer a girl but neither was I a wife. With this thought buzzing in my head, we started home to 69th Street, back where it all began.

THE END

Jean in prom dress, 1943.
Proceeds went to China relief fund.

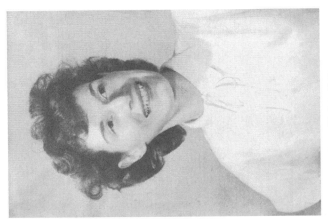

Sister Violet, 1940

Wes - Brooklyn, NY, 1940

Jean at Camp Shawangee, 1940

191

The ocelot coat.

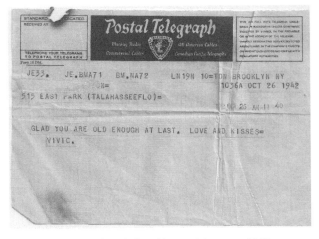

STANDARD | CATED
RECEIVED AT

Postal Telegraph

TELEPHONE YOUR TELEGRAMS
TO POSTAL TELEGRAPH

JE33.   JE.BMA71   BM.NA72   LN19N 10=TON BROOKLYN NY
                      N=   1036A OCT 26 1942
515 EAST PARK (TALAHASSEEFLO)=

GLAD YOU ARE OLD ENOUGH AT LAST. LOVE AND KISSES=
VIVIC.

Telegram about being old enough to marry, 1942.

Newlyweds: Wes and Jean, Jay and Meg - Tallahassee

Jean and Meg on Ford convertible - Tallahassee, Florida 1942

Wedding picture: Jean and Wes, Tallahassee, October 1942

Wes and Jean lining up for 19 cents a gallon gasoline, 1942

194

EPILOGUE

With Wes away on duty, Jean returned to college only to find it unproductive and unsatisfying. She felt she, too, had to do her part to contribute to the war effort. Jean found employment with Sperry Gyroscope at the Brooklyn Navy Yard. Her assignment was coordinator between Production Control and Manufacturing Information in the blueprint department. This required 6 days and 54 hours a week of bird-dogging blueprint changes from engineering to the machining floors. In her denim overalls and pinned back hair, she created a bit of a stir among the male workers. However, most of the men were 4F so they respected Jean's position as a wife of a combat pilot. After a hard day at the plant, it was home for dinner, write her nightly V-Mail and to bed. All her friends were off at school. The mother of her only remaining friend would not allow her to fraternize with a married woman.

Wes completed 98 missions and became an Ace, downing five enemy aircraft in the air and six on the ground. He was returning from a mission over Germany and had several bombs still aboard when he flew over Orly Airport in France. The German planes were so tempting to him that he disobeyed orders to proceed to base. He signaled his squadron to drop whatever they had left on the sitting ducks below. On the same day he was awarded a Presidential citation for this mission, he was brought up for an official reprimand.

The squadrons had been promised a leave after completion of their prescribed missions, but were suddenly told it would not be forthcoming. This did not sit well with Wes, so he went through channels all the way to General Eisenhower's headquarters in London, pleading his case. He obtained a 30-day pass with orders to report to Atlantic City for reevaluation of flight status.

By January, Jean had resigned her job at the plant. She and her family, after the Christmas rush at the store, took a week's vacation at a mountain resort. She had no idea Wes had succeeded in getting his leave and was surprised when he called from New York City to say he was stateside and coming up to join them. The reunion turned out to be disappointing and troublesome for both. Wes could not adjust to the abrupt change from his wartime experience to the abundance and complacency of so-called normal living. Jean, on the other hand, had expected someone she could lean on after her long year of solitude. Neither could fulfill the other's expectations.

When they got back to the city, Wes took Jean on a shopping spree. He had a long list of feminine articles that he said his commander had asked him to purchase for his wife. Jean helped him pick out nylons at Bloomingdales. At Elizabeth Arden, it was a full line of cosmetics and perfumes.

After many days of physical and mental testing in Atlantic City, it was determined Wes had Pilot's Fatigue. He would not be permitted to return to combat but, instead, he was to be assigned as an instructor at a base in Scotland. All available personnel were needed as D- DAY was fast approaching. Jean and Wes parted, unsure of their marriage, but promised to continue daily correspondence in the attempt to recreate a bond.

There was no telling when the war would end. At this time Jean decided to proceed on her longtime desire to go to Cornell. She applied for Home Economics thinking it would help her become a better wife. However, it was open only to women who lived on farms and would benefit the war effort. What was left was Russian Civilization and Journalism. She became a student in all ways. She never took off her wedding ring but took advantage of the many campus activities that she had missed out on previously. At last, her real self was emerging. All the branches of the military were taking classes under the V8 program so there were many opportunities to go to dances and events.

After enjoying a year of growth and freedom, Jean learned that Wes' tour of duty had concluded. He wired that he was on his way home. He would arrive in Boston, buy a car, and drive up to Ithaca. Jean had many mixed emotions. She treasured her new way of life and was fearful of what may lie ahead.

The day came when he was to arrive. Jean sat nervously in expectation on the lawn outside the sorority house while all the girls hung out the windows awaiting a glimpse of Wes. They were not disappointed when a very handsome officer drove up in a Buick convertible in full dress uniform--his chest covered with ribbons.

They tried to make a go of it, but never seemed to achieve what they had hoped. Wes received several short-term assignments uprooting them frequently. It was becoming very difficult for Jean to adjust. During one of their many disagreements, Wes accused her of having no backbone. He then confronted her with an 8x10 photo of the RAF's wife he had been dating in England while her husband was a POW. Here was someone who braved the Blitz, he said, and faced real challenges. He was sure to clarify to Jean that the items they shopped for when he was on leave had been meant for the English woman and not the commander's wife.

By the time the subject of divorce came up, Jean was pregnant. Returning to her parent's home was not an option. A son was born before the war ended. For five years, Wes could not find a suitable niche. They moved from New York to Miami and here a daughter was born. The saving grace came with the Korean War when Wes was recalled to stateside duty. Becoming an officer again and returning to flight status reestablished his self-esteem. What followed was fifteen years of military service, and 3 years overseas in Germany and France. Six years were spent at Patrick Air Force base at Cape Canaveral where Wes tracked fired missiles down range.

During these years, and despite occasional objections from Wes, Jean took on many new projects. In Germany, she was part of the formation of the first German-American Women's Club; President of the newly formed Toastmistress Club; delegate to the first women's conference in Bertchesgarten. She organized children's events and produced musical revues for the Officer's Clubs in Germany, France, and later PAFB, Fla. In Florida, Jean became a correspondent for 3 major newspapers. Their final military assignment was in California. Wes was assigned to the Missile Test Center at Lockheed.

They bought a house and it was the first time Jean could feel like a part of a community instead of a "dependent". She joined the PTA, wrote a newsletter for a newly projected hospital and wrote a column for the local newspaper.

After 3 years, Wes' military days came to an end. It was then he decided to move the family to the Virgin Islands. Jean was totally against it, but he was adamant that a tourist attraction needed to be built there and he was the one to do it. He acquired financial backing and despite huge misgivings, they relocated to St. Thomas. The enterprise was not successful through his efforts due to many local complications. This 3-year adventure resulted in divorce, twenty-three years in the making.

It would seem reasonable that Jean and her daughter would go back to her family in New York, but she had other plans. California called to her as San Francisco had called to her father so many years ago. After a visit with her family, she and her 15-year-old daughter set out for a new life in California.

Jean worked as the manager of a women's department store. A loving couple had taken her under their wings upon her return. Her dear friends took it upon themselves to introduce her to a man named Woodie. He had been a widower for six years. They were sure that he and Jean would be a good combination. It took one year to arrange a casual meeting. The morning after their first introduction, Helen called to see how it went. In her clipped British accent she said, "He's very nice, but he's probably not your type." When Jean hung up, she mused, "What is my type? Certainly not the same top-gun personality I was used to." She soon realized Woodie was the kindest, most considerate man she had ever met, besides being strong and athletic.

One year later, they were married. Jean had a "real wedding," with church bells and rice. Their choice of home turned out to be 2 blocks from where she used to live. She was able to go to Foothill College and get a degree in Travel Careers; write a column for a local newspaper; and take creative writing at DeAnza College. She was blessed with a wonderful husband of 44 amazing years; a stepdaughter, her 2 children, 2 grandchildren and finally, after so many years, a lovely home with a sloping lawn, a friendly neighborhood, and a tree lined street.

Sitting on a bench at Cornell University. It says,
"To those who sit here rejoicing, To those who sit here mourning,
Sympathy and greeting: So have we done in our time. 1892"

ACKNOWLEDGEMENTS

What started out as a series of vignettes of my childhood, gradually became a book due to the encouragement of fellow writers who kept asking for one more chapter.

In the twenty years of gestation, I am grateful for the creative outlets I have been fortunate enough to be part of.

For the two incredible workshops: first with Carole Davis, Creative writing Instructor at De Anza College in Cupertino and the inspiring classmates; and the participants of the Writer's Workshop 1990-1998 at Lake Wildwood, Penn Valley,CA — many thanks.

For bringing the book to fruition, the following were indispensable: Meg Foard, Publishing Consultant and Graphic Designer and Judee Humburg, Oral Historian with Stanford Historical Society, and Full Circle Stories Publishing, two amazing women who led me through the maze of self-publishing.

Then when I thought I was finally done making corrections and additions (enough already), my daughters, Judee Humburg and Leara Clausing — writer, entertainer (who is also amazing) forced me to take it a step further to make positive changes — for that I am truly grateful.

Also, as she would phrase it, a shout out at Karen Grimshaw and her love for commas and her aversion to run on sentences. Also to Lew Istre, grammarian extraordinaire.

Lastly, to my parents, Elvira and William, for giving me such a colorful history to share — I love you for it.

THE AUTHOR

Jean Humburg lives in a small town in the Sierra Foothills. She is the author of two books, "Honk if You Like Canada Geese," and "Honk Again," humorous essays on coping with life in general.

She was a columnist for the local paper and for many years conducted a writer's workshop. She has dabbled in all that is creative, enjoying life to the fullest.

Made in the USA
San Bernardino, CA
20 November 2013